Impressions 1

America Through Academic Readings

HomeWork
134 - 139
6, 7 8 9

December 11

Impressions 1

America Through Academic Readings

Cheryl Benz
Georgia Perimeter College

Stephen Benz
Georgia Perimeter College

THOMSON

HEINLE

Australia • Canada • Mexico • Singapore • Spain • United Kingdom • United States

Impressions 1: America Through Academic Readings
Cheryl Benz & Stephen Benz

Publisher: *Sherrise Roehr*
Acquisitions Editor: *Tom Jefferies*
Director of Content Development: *Anita Raducanu*
Director of Product Marketing: *Amy Mabley*
Executive Marketing Manager: *Jim McDonough*
Associate Production Editor: *John Sarantakis*

Manufacturing Manager: *Marcia Locke*
Production Project Manager: *Lois Lombardo*
Photo Researcher: *Poyee Oster*
Cover Designer: *Lori Stuart*
Composition: *Nesbitt Graphics, Inc.*
Printer: *West Group*

Cover Image: Jupiter Images

Printed in the United States of America.
1 2 3 4 5 6 7 8 9 10   11 10 09 08 07

For more information contact Thomson Heinle, 25
Thomson Place, Boston, Massachusetts 02210 USA, or
you can visit our Internet site at elt.thomson.com

ISBN-13: 978-0-618-41026-2
ISBN-10: 0-618-41026-0
ISE ISBN-13: 978-1-4240-1737-9
ISE ISBN-10: 1-4240-1737-8

Credits appear on pages 149–150, which constitute a
continuation of the copyright page.

Library of Congress Control Number: 2007923312

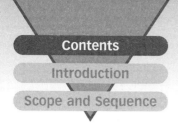

Contents

Introduction   xi

Scope and Sequence   xvii

CHAPTER 1   **VALUES AND IMPRESSIONS**   **1**

Overall Impressions   **Reading 1**   **2**
American Culture and Values   **3**
Reading Skills   5
Vocabulary Skills   7
Discussion Activities   10
Reading-Response Journal   11
Writing Topics   11

In-Depth Impressions   **Reading 2**   **12**
The American Value of Individualism   **13**
Reading Skills   15
Vocabulary Skills   16
Discussion Activities   18
Reading-Response Journal   19
Writing Topics   19

Student Impressions   **Keeping to the Tradition**   **20**

Personal Impressions   **Reading 3**   **22**
John Muir and Conflicting American Values   **23**
Reading Skills   26
Vocabulary Skills   27
Discussion Activities   29
Reading-Response Journal   29
Writing Topics   29
Internet Activities   29

CHAPTER 2   THE AMERICAN IDIOM   31

Overall Impressions   **Reading 1**   32
Languages in the United States   33
Reading Skills   36
Vocabulary Skills   37
Discussion Activities   40
Reading-Response Journal   41
Writing Topics   41

Student Impressions   **The Swahili Language**   42

In-Depth Impressions   **Reading 2**   43
African American Vernacular English   44
Reading Skills   46
Vocabulary Skills   47
Discussion Activities   49
Reading-Response Journal   49
Writing Topics   50

Personal Impressions   **Reading 3**   51
Walt Whitman: A Man of Words   52
Reading Skills   54
Vocabulary Skills   55
Discussion Activities   56
Reading-Response Journal   57
Writing Topics   57
Internet Activities   57

CHAPTER 3   IMMIGRANT IMPRESSIONS   59

Overall Impressions   **Reading 1**   60
Immigration in the United States   61
Reading Skills   65
Vocabulary Skills   68
Discussion Activities   70
Reading-Response Journal   70

Student Impressions   **It Takes Courage!**   70
Writing Topic   72

In-Depth Impressions | **Reading 2**   74
Who Belongs to "Generation 1.5"?   75
Reading Skills   78
Vocabulary Skills   80
Discussion Activities   82
Reading-Response Journal   83
Writing Topics   83

Personal Impressions | **Reading 3**   84
Leonid Yelin: An Immigrant's Story   85
Reading Skills   88
Vocabulary Skills   88
Discussion Activities   90
Reading-Response Journal   91
Writing Topics   91
Internet Activities   91

CHAPTER 4   GEOGRAPHY AND CULTURE IN THE UNITED STATES   93

Overall Impressions | **Reading 1**   94
Road Trip, USA   95
Reading Skills   98
Vocabulary Skills   99
Discussion Activities   102
Reading-Response Journal   102

Student Impressions | **Students Reflect on America's Car Culture**   103
Writing Topics   104

In-Depth Impressions | **Reading 2**   105
Myths of the American West   106
Reading Skills   108
Vocabulary Skills   109
Discussion Activities   111
Reading-Response Journal   111
Writing Topics   111

Personal Impressions   **Reading 3**   **112**
Memoir of a Road Trip   113
Reading Skills   114
Vocabulary Skills   115
Discussion Activities   117
Reading-Response Journal   117
Writing Topics   117
Internet Activites   117

CHAPTER 5   MUSICAL IMPRESSIONS   119

Overall Impressions   **Reading 1**   **120**
American Music   121
Reading Skills   125
Vocabulary Skills   128
Discussion Activities   131
Reading-Response Journal   131
Writing Topics   131

Student Impressions   **Traditional Music Is Best**   **132**

In-Depth Impressions   **Reading 2**   **133**
The Emergence of Hip-Hop   134
Reading Skills   135
Vocabulary Skills   137
Discussion Activities   139
Reading-Response Journal   139
Writing Topics   140

Personal Impressions   **Reading 3**   **141**
Louis Armstrong: America's Musical Ambassador   142
Reading Skills   143
Vocabulary Skills   144

Discussion Activities   146
Reading-Response Journal   146
Writing Topics   146
Internet Activities   147

Credits   149
Vocabulary Index   151
Skills Index   155

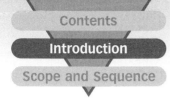

Contents

Introduction

Scope and Sequence

Introduction

Impressions uses academic readings to encourage students to explore their impressions of American culture. The series emphasizes academic skills appropriate for students who intend to go in to higher education programs. The two-book series includes readings on various aspects of American culture. A variety of exercises accompany each reading. These exercises enable students to understand the readings, to improve their vocabulary, to discuss issues with each other, and to write about what they have learned.

PURPOSE OF *IMPRESSIONS*

People learn languages in different ways and for different reasons. One of the most difficult tasks a language learner can undertake is the pursuit of higher education in a language other than one's own. Many people achieve competency in another language for the purposes of travel, employment, or casual communication. But even those who attain a degree of fluency in daily usage can find attending university-level courses a more daunting challenge. Students who need to learn English for academic purposes face numerous difficulties. In academic discourse, grammatical constructions are more sophisticated and vocabulary is more technical. Students are expected to recognize and employ particular rhetorical conventions. Reading comprehension depends on advanced skills in inference and attention to <u>nuances</u> and connotations. Many English-language learners have had only limited experience in the distinct academic culture that prevails in American institutions of higher education, yet their success often depends on their ability to master this culture. Simply put, English-language learners in American institutions of higher education have to learn much more than the surface features of the language.

Impressions attempts to address these needs by helping students develop the linguistic, rhetorical, and critical thinking skills necessary for successful participation in colleges and universities. The readings in this series approximate the kinds of reading encountered in college courses. Moreover, the readings focus on culture and values in the United States, in part to help students achieve a level of cultural literacy and in part to introduce students to some of the issues frequently addressed in U.S. college courses. The exercises and activities in each chapter focus on the language skills necessary for academic success.

ORGANIZATION OF READING SELECTIONS

It is impossible to cover all aspects of American culture in depth within the scope of this series. Reading topics have been chosen based on students' need for exposure to real-word and academic aspects of U.S. culture. The readings are designed to advance students from a precollege reading level in Book 1 (levels 8-11) to college level in Book 2.

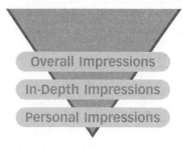

Arranged thematically, each chapter of *Impressions* revolves around a different aspect of U.S. culture. Within each chapter, the reading selections are arranged from a general overview to a more specific and more personal aspect of each theme. The first reading selection in each chapter is designated *Overall Impressions*, the second is *In-Depth Impressions*, and the final selection is *Personal Impressions*. Thus students are led on a logical progression through each theme. This structure is highlighted by the triangle icon that accompanies each reading selection.

Supplemental activities and links to information germane to the reading selections in the book can be found on the *Impressions* website **elt.thomson.com/impressions**

LANGUAGE SKILLS

As noted earlier, the exercises and activities in each chapter focus on the language skills necessary for academic success. These exercises and activities provide practice in prereading, reading comprehension skills, vocabulary skills, interactive reading strategies, oral activities and group work, and writing activities based on the reading selections.

Prereading Activities

According to H. Douglas Brown (1994), "The reader brings information, knowledge, emotion, experience, and culture to the printed word." (p. 284). A primary key to improving students' reading comprehension is to use their background knowledge and encourage them to think about what they already know about a topic before they begin reading. The prereading activities in *Impressions* include discussion questions and prediction activities meant to activate students' schemata before they begin the reading selection. This section also includes a preview of vocabulary words that will help students' reading comprehension.

Reading Skills

Understanding text is the primary goal of reading. The exercises after each reading selection are meant to assess students' reading comprehension. They focus on helping students learn how to (1) identify the main idea of a reading passage and (2) skim and scan texts in order to answer questions about details. In addition to strengthening students' reading comprehension, these exercises prepare students for the types of questions that appear on standardized reading tests. Furthermore, academic reading comprehension depends on advanced skills in inference and attention to nuances and connotations. *Impressions* also includes reading comprehension exercises that exercise these higher-level thinking skills.

Vocabulary Skills

Keith Folse (2004) asserts, "Vocabulary is perhaps the most important component in second language ability" (p. 22). For many years, ESL teachers have applied research about how native speakers learn vocabulary words to their non-native-speaking students. However, more recent research shows that non-native speakers learn vocabulary differently than native speakers. For example, contrary to popular belief, learning lists of vocabulary words is a productive way for non-native speakers to learn new vocabulary. Also effective is repeated contact with new vocabulary words in a variety of contexts—in other words, the more students come into contact with and use the new vocabulary words, the more likely they are to remember them. One very effective way to encourage this is through a vocabulary notebook. The how and why of creating a vocabulary notebook are explained on page 7. Additionally, the vocabulary exercises in *Impressions* give special attention to collocations. Collocations are words or phrases that work together to form natural-sounding speech or writing. For example, in English one can commit murder, but one cannot commit a joke. For both comprehension and production of the language, students need to learn specific collocations, especially those common to academic English.

Another important feature in this text is the focus on academic words. Academic vocabulary involves two kinds of words: general academic words and technical words that are used for a particular academic discipline. In this textbook, general academic words are addressed through the use of the Academic Word List (AWL) developed by Averil Coxhead (2000). AWL words are used frequently in all academic disciplines from mathematics to humanities and everything in between. Because these words cut across academic disciplines, focusing on AWL words will help students become more proficient readers in any academic discipline. A list of AWL words, which for simplicity we refer to throughout the series as Academic Words, follows each reading selection. To reinforce previous encounters with these words, they are divided into lists of new words and words that students have encountered in previous reading selections.

Technical words are addressed in the *Previewing Specialized Vocabulary* section that precedes each reading selection. Knowing the meaning of these words may help students understand the reading selection better; they are not included in the vocabulary development section, however, because they do not occur with great frequency in academic texts.

Group Activities

Some students learn best through oral activities and group interaction; however, not all group activities and group interactions are equally beneficial to students. Group activities must be meaningful and ensure the participation of all members. Page 10 in this book features an activity that encourages students to consider what it means to be an effective group member. As part of this activity, students create their own rules for being a good group member. These student-created rules are referred to in all later group activities, under the heading *Discussion Activities*.

Group activities are also important for non-native-speaking students because it is an instructional method often employed in American academic classes. Each chapter provides students with practice in a group activity in order to better prepare them for teaching methods they may not have encountered in their first-language education.

Reading Journal

What do "good readers" do to improve comprehension and retain what they have read? They interact with the text. They note what is most important, what is original, what is clear or unclear. They relate the text to their own experiences or something they have read before. In this book, the *Reading-Response Journal* activities guide students in becoming interactive readers. For this reason, the *Reading-Response Journal* questions are focused differently than the reading comprehension exercises. By keeping a reading journal, students practice being interactive readers and critical thinkers—skills that will serve them well in future encounters with academic texts.

Writing Topics

In academic classes, students are often asked to write about what they read. They are expected to recognize and employ the rhetorical conventions used in academic settings. The writing topics in this text are meant to increase critical thinking and mirror the types of writing assignments students might be asked to do in American academic classes. One special feature of *Impressions* is original student writing. The *Student Impressions* section of each chapter highlights a student text focused on the theme covered in each chapter. These texts can be used as models for student writing or to help students generate ideas in order to respond to the writing of their peers.

WEB-BASED SUPPLEMENTS

The student website **elt.thomson.com/impressions** offers students supplemental activities, including vocabulary flash cards and quizzes.

ACKNOWLEDGMENTS

The authors wish to express their thanks to Susan Maguire for her guidance, support, and insight in the developmental stages of this project. Evangeline Bermas and Joann Kozyrev also lent their expertise in making this book a reality. Our special thanks and deepest gratitude go to developmental editor Kathy Sands Boehmer, whose diligence, enthusiasm, and patience kept the project on track through difficulties and tribulations.

The following reviewers contributed valuable advice and practical comments:

Anne Bachmann, Clackamas Community College

Michael D'Entremont, Bunker Hill Community College

Mark Ende, Onondaga Community College

Laurie Moody, Passaic Community College

Leslie Reichert, City College of San Francisco

Audrey Short, Bronx Community College

Christine Tierney, Houston Community College.

We are indebted to colleagues, particularly at Georgia Perimeter College, for their support and advice. Finally, we thank the students who have been in our classes over the years. Their persistence in pursuit of their hopes and dreams has continually inspired and motivated us.

References

Brown, H.D. (1994). *Teaching by principles.* Upper Saddle River: Prentice Hall Regents.

Coxhead, A. (2000). A new academic word list. *TESOL Quarterly 34*(2), 213-238.

Folse, K.S. (2004). *Vocabulary myths.* Ann Arbor: The University of Michigan Press.

Scope and Sequence

CHAPTER	READINGS	READING SKILLS	VOCABULARY SKILLS
1 Values and Impressions	American Culture and Values The American Value of Individualism John Muir and Conflicting American Values	Preparing to read by prereading, predicting, and previewing specialized vocabulary Finding the main idea and details that support that idea Finding specific details to answer questions Making a connection between personal experiences and reading topics Expressing an opinion by discussing and by writing about the readings	Learning new vocabulary words commonly found in academic texts Keeping a vocabulary notebook Discovering word forms Practicing with verbs followed by prepositions Understanding collocations
2 The American Idiom	Languages in the United States African American Vernacular English Walt Whitman: A Man of Words	Prereading, predicting, and previewing specialized vocabulary Finding the main idea in a reading Reviewing for specific details Reading diagrams Making a connection between personal experiences and reading topics Expressing an opinion by discussing and by writing about the readings Reading poetry	Learning new Academic Words Acquiring and expanding dictionary skills Recognizing acronyms Distinguishing nouns in the same noun family
3 Immigrant Impressions	Immigration in the United States Who Belongs to "Generation 1.5"? Leonid Yelin: An Immigrant's Story	Prereading, predicting, and previewing specialized vocabulary Finding the main idea of a reading Organizing and ordering details Reading a graph Recognizing figurative language Making a connection between personal experiences and reading topics Expressing an opinion by discussing and by writing about the readings	Learning new Academic Words Studying word parts Differentiating commonly confused words Improving fluency with collocations
4 Geography and Culture in the United States	Road Trip, USA Myths of the American West Memoir of a Road Trip	Prereading, predicting, and previewing specialized vocabulary Finding the main idea Finding specific details in a reading Reading maps Distinguishing fact from opinion Expressing opinions in an academic setting Making a connection between personal experiences and reading topics Expressing an opinion by discussing and by writing about the readings	Learning new Academic Words Practicing with adjectives Recognizing opposites Using phrasal verbs Reviewing word forms Recognizing related words
5 Musical Impressions	American Music The Emergence of Hip-Hop Louis Armstrong: America's Musical Ambassador	Prereading, predicting, and previewing specialized vocabulary Acknowledging the ideas of others Using headings to remember details Sequencing details Making a connection between personal experiences and reading topics Expressing an opinion by discussing and by writing about the readings	Learning new Academic Words Using the dictionary to distinguish between noun and verb forms Understanding collocations with adverbs Using context clues for better vocabulary comprehension Recognizing idiomatic phrases

Values and Impressions

Values are the ideas we think are important. We show what is important, what we value, by the way we act. Understanding values can help us understand people's actions. For example, people who value their family spend time doing family activities. They help family members when they have problems. In this chapter, you will read about American culture and values and how these values influence the way Americans act.

> ❝A new world is not made simply by trying to forget the old. A new world is made with a new spirit, with new values.❞
>
> —Henry Miller,
> American author

> ❝The values upon which our system is built . . . imply our adherence not only to liberty and individual freedom, but also to international peace, law and order, and constructive social purpose. When we depart from these values, we do so at our peril.❞
>
> —William Fulbright,
> U.S. senator

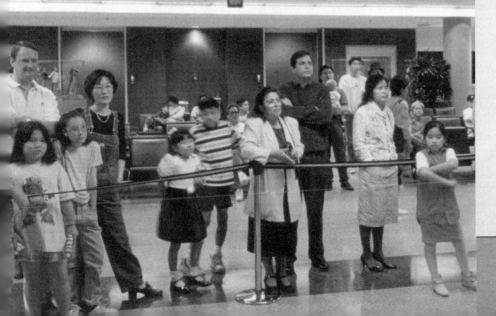

Overall Impressions

READING 1

Prereading

Before you read, discuss the following questions with your classmates.

1. What is culture?

2. What are values?

3. What are some things that Americans value?

4. How are American values different from values of people from other countries?

Predicting

Predicting can help you understand what you read. Before you read, do the following activities. They will help you predict what the reading selection will be about.

1. Study the charts in this chapter. What kind of information is in the charts?

2. What do you think this reading selection is about?

Previewing Specialized Vocabulary

Listed here are some of the specialized words that you will find in this reading selection. Knowing and understanding these words will help you understand the reading selection better.

- Review the definitions of these words.
- Identify which of these words, if any, you already know.
- Try to paraphrase the meaning of each word.
- Underline these words in the reading selection.

ingrained (*adj.*)—built in, deep-rooted (paragraph 6)

competitive (*adj.*)—aggressive, wanting to be the winner (paragraph 6)

informal (*adj.*)—not formal, casual (paragraph 6)

generalize (*v.*)—to oversimplify, take a broad view (paragraph 7)

mainstream culture (*n. ph.*)—the culture of most of the people, the normal way of acting (paragraph 8)

subculture (*n.*)—the culture of a small number of people, not considered normal by most of the people (paragraph 8)

heritage (*n.*)—tradition, custom (paragraph 8)

upheld (*v.*)—supported, defended (paragraph 9)

celebrates (*v.*)—pays honor to (paragraph 13)

American Culture and Values

What Is Culture?

1   In general, the term *culture* refers to a set of customs, traditions, and behaviors common to a particular human society. There is no generally accepted definition of *culture*. However, most social scientists use the word to describe all of the behavioral patterns, beliefs, institutions, and products of a particular population.

CHART 1.1   WHAT ARE SOME ELEMENTS OF CULTURE?

- Behavioral patterns (example: the way different people think about time)
- Beliefs (example: belief in one god)
- Institutions (example: trial by jury)
- Products (example: folk music)

---

2   In this book, you are going to read about some elements of culture in the United States. You are going to learn about some of the behavioral patterns, beliefs, institutions, and cultural products of people living in the United States of America.

Why It Is Important to Learn About Values

3   The United States can be confusing to a visitor from another country. It is difficult for someone who has just arrived to understand why Americans act the way they do. In any culture, the way people act reflects the things they think are important. Whatever people think is important shapes their values. People in one culture may think it is important to show respect to elderly people. Those people value the wisdom that comes from living for a long time. In another culture, people may value youth. Those people value the energy and new ideas that come from young people.

4   Each year, thousands of people from all around the world come to the United States. Some visit as tourists; others come to do business. Many visitors are students who have come to study in American schools and universities. Still others are looking for a new life.

One Idea About American Values: Robert Kohls

5   At some point, many of these people will take classes to help them improve their English. They also want to improve their understanding of life in the United States. Students in such programs often learn about American values. For example, in some programs, they read a description of American values written by L. Robert Kohls, who served as director of the Washington International Center.

6   Kohls says that to make sense of another culture, we must understand "the basic beliefs, assumptions, and values of that particular group." To help foreign visitors make sense of American behaviors, Kohls has identified thirteen basic values. Chart 1.2 shows eight of Kohls's basic values. He says that these values are "deeply ingrained" in most Americans. According to Kohls, understanding American values will help foreign visitors understand "95% of American actions." Some foreigners might find these actions strange, confusing, or unbelievable because they are used to different beliefs, assumptions, and values. Look at these eight values. With a

partner, discuss what you think they mean. Can you think of other examples of each value?

CHART 1.2	AMERICAN VALUES: ROBERT KOHLS
Value	**Examples (Common Actions of Americans That Reflect Their Values)**
Personal control over the environment	Most American homes have central heating and air conditioning. Some Americans are very uncomfortable if they cannot control the temperature around them.
Change	Most Americans prefer new things and new ways of doing things. They usually buy a new car every three or four years. They like to have the latest technology in their homes.
Time and its control	Most Americans like things to begin on time. Business meetings usually begin and end on time.
Equality	Most Americans believe that people should be treated equally. Men and women should be treated the same, especially at work. It is accepted for women to work as doctors or construction workers and for men to work as secretaries or housecleaners.
Individualism	People can act as they choose to, as long as their actions do not hurt another person. Most Americans believe that it is important to be recognized as an individual rather than part of a group.
Competition	Many Americans are competitive. In school, students compete to get the best grade in the class.
Informality	Americans are generally informal. Even in some businesses, Americans dress in informal clothes.
Materialism	Most Americans like to own nice things. They usually own a car, one or more TVs, and a computer.

7   Not everyone agrees with Kohls. Some people say that it is impossible to generalize about a nation with a population of 300 million. While many people do believe in "personal control over the environment," others do not. Some Americans are materialistic. Many others are not. In other words, it is rather difficult to describe a common culture for such a diverse society. Does the United States have a single culture? Are there behaviors, beliefs, and values that all Americans share? Or is American society just too diverse to describe in generalizations? What—and who—can qualify as "truly American"?

Mainstream Culture and Subculture

8   Some scholars argue that the United States has many subcultures. Other scholars argue that a *mainstream culture* shapes the institutions that control the beliefs and values of people in the United States. Much of the mainstream culture comes from traditional European ideas. But scholars recognize that this mainstream culture has been influenced by Native Americans, by Africans who were brought to

the United States as slaves, and by other more recent immigrants from Asia, the Americas, and elsewhere. It is clear that the cultural heritage of the United States includes elements from every part of the world. This means that many perspectives exist side by side.

Actions Speak Louder than Words

9   Because the United States is a large country with citizens who come from many different parts of the world, we cannot speak of a single American culture. We can, however, identify some of the values that are generally upheld in American culture. Most Americans know that these *stated* ideals are not always put into practice. The meaning of these ideals is subject to continuing discussion. The nation's history has many conflicts in values and actions. For example, Americans have not always treated one another equally or respectfully. Some people in the United States have suffered when others looked down on them. Often conflict arises among Americans when one group fails to pay attention to the values that most Americans think are important.

10   It is easy to say, "I value or believe in" one thing or another. Sometimes people who say they believe something act in the opposite way. Americans like to say, "Actions speak louder than words." What do the actions of Americans tell us about their beliefs and values?

Another Idea About American Values: Robert Bellah

11   The anthropologist Robert Bellah agrees with Kohls that Americans share a common culture. According to Bellah, this common culture comes from the nation's institutions, including schools and government. He says that people who do not agree with mainstream values in the United States are often poor or live in neighborhoods that are separated from the rest of American society.

12   One way in which mainstream culture separates people is through an emphasis on individualism. Bellah says that the belief in individualism is powerful. It is so powerful that sometimes Americans pay too much attention to individual goals. He believes that individualism can have a bad effect on Americans. They do not show concern for other people or what is best for other people. Bellah thinks that Americans are too individualistic. He says that in such a system, only a small number of people can be winners. These few people will have most of the money, power, and freedom. Everyone else loses.

13   Bellah's concern about the bad effects of individualism is not important to many Americans. They believe that self-interest leads to the best result both for the individual and for society as a whole. American culture celebrates the ideal of individualism. But as Bellah's careful analysis shows, even the most celebrated of ideals can cause disagreement.

READING SKILLS

| EXERCISE 1 | **Finding the Main Idea** |

To understand the main idea of a reading selection, it is important to understand the reason why it was written. Choose the main purpose of this reading selection from the choices given. Explain why you think your choice is the best answer.

What is the main purpose of this reading selection?

    a. to explain why Americans need values

    b. to explain why Americans act so strangely

    c. to explain eight American values identified by Robert Kohls

    d. to explain some different ideas about American values

EXERCISE **2**   ## Reading for Details

Choose the correct answer based on the reading selection.

1. Showing respect to elderly people is an example of

    a. a culture.   b. a value.

    c. a belief.   d. a behavioral pattern.

2. According to Robert Kohls, to understand another culture we need to

    a. understand the values of that group.

    b. understand the assumptions of that group.

    c. understand the beliefs of that group.

    d. understand the values, assumptions, and beliefs of that group.

3. A foreigner might find Americans strange because

    a. sometimes Americans' actions do not reflect their values.

    b. Americans like competition and individualism.

    c. a foreigner might be used to different beliefs, assumptions, and values.

    d. 95 percent of Americans' actions come from their values.

4. Which is not an example of an American value from Chart 1.2?

    a. Most Americans like things to start on time.

    b. Most Americans believe that it is important to cooperate with others.

    c. Most Americans like to buy and own nice things.

    d. Most Americans believe that it is important to be better than other people.

5. All Americans agree with Kohls's ideas about American values.

    a. True   b. False

6. Mainstream American culture is influenced by

    a. traditional European ideas along with those of Native Americans, Africans, and immigrants.

    b. only traditional European ideas.

    c. mostly Native Americans, Africans, and immigrants.

    d. traditional European ideas and immigrants from Asia and the Americas.

7. American values are always reflected in their actions.

    a. True   b. False

8. According to Robert Bellah, people who are poor or live in neighborhoods separated from the rest of American society

    a. are usually part of mainstream American culture.

    b. are usually part of a subculture.

    c. usually have the most power and freedom.

    d. are usually the small number of people who are winners.

VOCABULARY SKILLS

EXERCISE 3   **Academic Word List**

The following words are frequently found in academic writing. Knowing these words will help you read all kinds of academic texts. There are many ways to learn new vocabulary words. Each reading selection will have suggestions on how you can learn the Academic Words. Try the different suggestions until you find the one that works the best for you. The number in parentheses indicates the paragraph in this reading selection where the word appears.

1. culture (1), cultural (2), subculture (8)

2. traditions (1)

3. definition (1)

4. institutions (1)

5. elements (1)

6. energy (3)

7. assumptions (6)

8. identified (6), identify (9)

9. chart (6)

10. environment (6)

11. individual (6), individualism (6), individualistic (10)

12. grade (6)

13. computer (6)

14. diverse (7)

15. immigrants (8)

16. perspectives (8)

17. conflict (9)

18. goals (12)

19. analysis (13)

EXERCISE 4   **Vocabulary Notebook**

Keeping a vocabulary notebook is a good way to learn vocabulary words, because it gives you an opportunity to easily review the words. It is important to organize the vocabulary notebook neatly. You might organize it in alphabetical order. This will help you practice the words many times. For each word, include these pieces of information:

- the word
- a short definition or its opposite
- a brief example (a whole sentence is not necessary)

Here is an example:

Word	Definition	Example
analysis (n.)	examination of facts	careful analysis

You can use your vocabulary notebook to remind you of words you already know. You can also add more information about the word each time you read it in a different text. For example:

Word	Definition	Example
analysis (n.)	examination of facts	careful analysis
		carry out an analysis

EXERCISE 5

Discovering Related Word Forms

Once you learn a word, it is easy to learn related words. Learning related words is a good way to increase your vocabulary. Here are some of the words from the Academic Word List and related words. Practice pronouncing the words. Study the list. Then answer the questions that follow the list.

Noun	Verb	Adjective	Adverb
analysis	analyze	analytic	analytically
computer	compute	computerized	
conflict	conflict	conflicting	
contrast	contrast	contrasting	
cooperation	cooperate	cooperative	cooperatively
creation, creativity	create	creative	creatively
culture, subculture		cultural	culturally
definition	define	defined	
diversity, diversification	diversify	diverse	diversely
energy	energize	energetic, energized	energetically
environment		environmental	environmentally
individual, individualism, individuality	individualize	individualistic, individualized	individualistically
institution		institutional	institutionally
tradition		traditional	traditionally

1. Look at the adverb forms. What letters do they end in?

   _____ ly

2. Which words end in *ic*?

   a. _Analytic_   c. _Individuallistic_

   b. _Energetic_

3. Words ending in *ic* are usually what part of speech (noun, verb, adjective, adverb)? _Adjetive_

4. Which words end in *tion*?

a. _Cooperation_   d. _diversification_
b. _Creation_   e. _Institution_
c. _definition_   f. _Tradition_

5. Words ending in *tion* are usually what part of speech (noun, verb, adjective, adverb)? _Noun_

6. Which words end in *al*?

a. _Individual_   d. _Institutional_
b. _Cultural_   e. _Traditional_
c. _Enviromental_

7. Most of the words ending in *al* are what part of speech (noun, verb, adjective, adverb)? _Noun, Adjetives_

8. Which words end in *ed*?

a. _Computerized_   c. _Energized_
b. _defined_   d. _Individualized_

9. Words ending in *ed* are usually what part of speech (noun, verb, adjective, adverb)? _Adjetives_

10. What is another form that uses *ed*? _Past Tense_.

11. Which words end in *tive*?

a. _Cooperative_   b. _Creative_

12. Words ending in *tive* are usually what part of speech (noun, verb, adjective, adverb)? _Adjetive_

13. Which words end in *ity*?

a. _Creativity_   c. _Individuality_
b. _diversity_

14. Words ending in *ity* are usually what part of speech (noun, verb, adjective, adverb)? _Noun_

15. Which words end in *ize* or *yze*?

a. _Analize_   c. _Individualize_

b. _Energize_   d. _____

16. Words ending in *ize* or *yze* are usually what part of speech (noun, verb, adjective, adverb)? _Verb._

17. Which words are the same in the noun and verb forms?

a. _Conflict_   b. _Contrast._

18. Words ending in *ly* are usually what part of speech (noun, verb, adjective, adverb)? _Adverbs._

DISCUSSION ACTIVITIES

Working with Groups

Many of the Discussion Activities in this text require group work. The purpose of this activity is for you and your classmates to develop rules for being a responsible group member. You will use these rules as you do the activities in the book. You should review the rules each time you do a group activity.

1. Write answers to the following questions:

a. Are you a shy or an outgoing person? Explain why you are shy or outgoing.

b. Did you ever work on a project with a group of students before? If the answer is yes, explain the project.

c. Was it a successful or an unpleasant group experience? Explain.

d. What are three things that good group members do?

2. Now work in a group of three or four students.

a. Arrange your desks or chairs in a circle so that you are all facing each other.

b. Introduce yourself. Make sure you know the name of each group member.

c. Tell your group members about your answers to the questions in Activity 1.

d. With your group, choose what you think are the five most important qualities of a good group member.

3. With your classmates, compile a list of qualities of good group members. Your teacher will post these rules in your classroom. These will be the rules that you will follow for group projects.

**Talking About
Your Own Values**

Practice the rules you have created for group activities by doing the following:

1. Look at Chart 1.1. With your group of four, list some other examples of elements of culture. Share your list with your other classmates.

2. Look at Chart 1.2. Think about your own values. Are they like American values? Make a mark by the American values that are similar to your values. Then explain to a partner why you chose to make your marks where you did. What kinds of things influenced your values? Your family? Friends? The country you came from? Your own personality? Compare your values to your partner's values.

READING-RESPONSE JOURNAL

The best readers think about what they read. One way to think about what you have read is to write about it. Choose one of the following topics, and write about it in your reading journal.

1. What information do you find interesting in this reading assignment? Summarize the point of interest, and then discuss why you find it interesting.

2. Choose one American value that you agree with. Explain why you agree. Choose another value that you do not agree with. Explain why you do not agree.

3. What do you think about Kohls's ideas? Do you think they accurately describe American values? Are there any values you would add? Are there any you think are less important to Americans than Kohls believes?

WRITING TOPICS

Choose one of the following topics, and write a composition.

1. How do Americans show what they value by the way they act? Write a composition describing two of Kohls's values that can be supported by the way Americans act. Give specific examples of actions you have observed.

2. Can you think of a place where some of the values that Kohls identifies are readily observed? For example, are these values on display in a shopping mall? A bank? An airport? A fast-food restaurant? A U.S. embassy or consulate? Write an essay describing how three of the values that Kohls identifies can be observed in one of these places. Describe the place in the first paragraph. In the following paragraphs, write about the values you can see there.

3. Bellah believes that individualism has a bad effect on American society. Do you agree or disagree with Bellah? Describe examples that support your opinion.

In-Depth Impressions

READING 2

Prereading

Before you read, discuss the following questions with your classmates.

1. What have you already learned about how Americans value individualism?

2. In your observations, how do Americans show that they value individualism?

Predicting

Before you read, do the following activities. They will help you predict what the reading selection will be about.

1. Look at the **bold** headings at the beginning of each section. What do you think each section will be about?

2. Look at the photos that go with this reading. Do you recognize any of the people or places in the photos? Use the pictures to predict what the reading selection will be about.

Previewing Specialized Vocabulary

Listed here are some of the specialized words that you will find in this reading selection. Knowing and understanding these words will help you understand the reading selection.

- Review the definitions of these words.
- Identify which of these words, if any, you already know.
- Try to paraphrase the meaning of each word.
- Underline these words in the reading selection.

frontier (*n.*)—the area beyond the places that people know well, especially in the western United States in the nineteenth century (paragraph 3)

anthropologist (*n.*)—a person who studies people, their societies, and their beliefs (paragraph 4)

rugged (*adj.*)—strong, healthy, vigorous (paragraph 8)

cowboy (*n.*)—a man who works on a cattle ranch (paragraph 8)

prospector (*n.*)—a person who searches for precious minerals or stones (paragraph 8)

frontiersman (*n.*)—a man who lives on the frontier and makes his living hunting or trapping animals (paragraph 8)

wilderness (*n.*)—wild, uncultivated land (paragraph 10)

The American Value of Individualism

1   One of the most important values in American culture is "individualism." A famous French political scientist, Alexis de Tocqueville, visited the United States in the middle of the nineteenth century. He wrote a book called *Democracy in America*. He was the first to describe Americans as individualistic. In the book, Tocqueville said that Americans tend to believe that people must help themselves and not rely on others for help. He called this belief individualism.

Reconocimiento — survey

2   Today, this term is familiar to most people. In surveys, Americans almost always express a strong preference for individual rather than group values. This does not mean that Americans don't like group activities. In fact, many Americans join clubs and are active in social groups. The emphasis on individualism means that Americans do not like to depend on others. They prefer to solve problems or make decisions for themselves.

3   Another trait of American individualism is distrust[1] of the government. Some political observers believe this distrust came from the frontier experience. The Americans who moved west to the wild frontier were cut off from the political system. Organized government was far away. As a result, people had to survive on their own. In such an environment, self-reliance and individualism became important.

Rasgo

Dependencia

Individualism in Everyday Life

4   Americans learn individualism at home and at school. Many elements of American culture support the idea that success is the result of individual effort. Francis Hsu, an American anthropologist, studied school systems in the United States. He found the idea of self-reliance to be typical of the American system. American children are taught to "go it alone." They must do their own work. They must solve problems by themselves. According to Hsu, this ideal is very different from the Asian ideal of group responsibility.

Esfuerzo

5   Visitors to the United States soon notice that Americans put great importance on individualism and self-reliance. Some newcomers may think that Americans are too extreme. In some cases, individualism can be more important than safety. For example, many Americans insist[2] that law-abiding citizens have a right to own a gun, even though guns can be dangerous to others in the community.

6   Other visitors think that children are spoiled by individualism. They think that American children are too assertive[3] and too free. Children do not always show respect to older people. To people from another cultural background, Americans sometimes seem to be rude or too impulsive[4].

7   One notable characteristic of America's individualistic culture is that young people are generally expected to leave home. During childhood, American children are prepared to leave home when they are eighteen years old. Americans often tend to look down on adults who live at home with their parents. Most Americans

[1]**to distrust** (*v.*) — lack of trust
[2]**to insist** (*v.*) — to claim that something is true.
[3]**assertive** (*adj.*) — acting overly confident in a way that draws people's attention
[4]**impulsive** (*adj.*) — tending to do things without thinking about the consequences

Impaciente – ilusionado
Entusiasmado

are eager to find employment that will allow them to be self-supporting. They want to take care of themselves without relying on their parents to do everything.

8   All in all, Americans like the idea of the "rugged individual." This is someone who can achieve great things through hard work. The cowboy, the lone prospector, and the frontiersman are just a few of the mythic embodiments of this ideal.

Encarnar – Exporchar

▲ John Wayne as a Hollywood cowboy

Individualism and Popular Culture

9   Popular culture also plays an important role in shaping American's view of individualism. The hero of popular Hollywood movies is often a "rugged individual." The perfect example of this is the cowboy. We often see cowboys in western movies fighting alone against evil. John Wayne became a famous movie star playing a rugged cowboy. More recently, Sylvester Stallone has updated the role as a gutsy boxer in his *Rocky* movies and as a soldier in his *Rambo* movies.

▲ Sylvester Stallone as Rocky

10   In TV commercials, we can see more examples of the individualistic spirit. Everything from soft drinks to cars is linked to the idea of individual freedom. The commercials suggest that a person can be an individual by drinking a certain cola or wearing certain clothes. Commercials for automobiles often show the car as the best way for a person to escape a busy life. Many commercials today show cars taking people far away. They drive into the wilderness, up mountains, or to deserted beaches.

11   To some scholars, there is a contradiction in these images. How can a soft drink express individuality if millions of people are drinking it? How can a car provide a means to escape society if its operation depends on roads and gas stations? In the end, the contradictions don't matter. Advertisers know that most Americans want to believe in the ideals of individualism. Americans will spend money to buy products that make them feel individualistic.

How Individualistic Are Americans?

12   Americans value individualism, but are they really individualistic? To many social scientists, peer groups have an important influence on Americans. Consider jeans, for example. What could be more American? But why do Americans dress all the same? Wearing the same outfit is not very individualistic. Americans have great freedom of choice when it comes to clothes. Still, the majority of people wear very similar clothing. Another example is the American political system. Americans have freedom of speech and religion. But there isn't much variety in mainstream American political ideas. For more than a century, there have been only two major political parties in the United States. Historically, the differences between those parties are not dramatic.

13   Similarly, most American cities have only one or two major daily newspapers. Indeed, across the country, all forms of media are remarkably similar. Radio stations play similar music in Seattle and Baltimore. News programs in Los Angeles and New York express similar ideas. In fact, a few large corporations own most of the television and radio stations in the United States. The result is a high degree of uniformity in content. This reality makes some people wonder about Americans. Do they just pay lip service to the idea of individualism, or is it truly a core value?

READING SKILLS

EXERCISE 6

Supporting the Main Idea with Examples

This reading selection has two main ideas:

1. Americans value individualism.

2. Americans are not as individualistic as they might believe.

There are several examples in the reading selection to support these ideas. Review the reading selection. Find examples that support each of the main ideas. Using highlighting pens of two different colors, mark the examples that support the main ideas.

EXERCISE 7

Looking for Details

Decide if each statement is true or false based on the reading selection. Write *T* if the sentence is true and *F* if it is false. If the sentence is false, change it to make the sentence true. The first one has been done for you as an example.

                                                                be individualistic.

__F__   **1.** According to Tocqueville, Americans tend to ~~depend on each other.~~

__T__   **2.** Most Americans do not like to depend on others to solve their problems and make their decisions.

__F__   **3.** Most Americans believe in individualism because they trust government.

__T__   **4.** Hsu found that the American school system focuses on individualism.

__F__   **5.** Hsu concluded that Americans are similar to Asians when it comes to individualism.

__T__   **6.** American individualism can cause misunderstandings between Americans and people from other cultures.

__T__   **7.** All American children are expected to leave home when they turn eighteen.

I **8.** The cowboy is a symbol of individualism.

F **9.** There are not many examples of individualism in American movies.

F **10.** Television commercials try to avoid showing individuality because they want people to buy all the same things.

F **11.** Americans may say they believe in individualism, but in many ways they are similar to each other.

EXERCISE 8

Relating Reading to Your Opinions and Experiences

One way to make sure you understand what you read is to discuss the reading selection with a partner. Another strategy that helps you understand is to connect what you read with your own experiences. Working with a partner, discuss your opinions on one or more of the following questions. Support your opinion with your background knowledge or experiences.

1. The reading suggests that many Americans distrust government. Do you agree or disagree with this statement? Why?

2. American schools teach children that they must do their own work. The Asian ideal of group responsibility encourages classmates to work together. Which do you think is a better way of teaching children? Why?

3. Many Americans believe that citizens have the right to own a gun. Do you think this is an important right? Why?

4. Do you think that American children are too assertive or free? In your view, are they rude or impulsive? Why?

5. Should children be encouraged to leave home when they are eighteen? Why?

VOCABULARY SKILLS

EXERCISE 9

Academic Word List

The following words are frequently found in academic writing. Knowing these words will help you read all kinds of academic texts. The first list is of Academic Words that you have seen earlier in this book. You can find these words again in this reading selection. Make sure these words are in your vocabulary notebook. (See page 7 for information about how to make a vocabulary notebook.) Add any new information that you learn about these words to your vocabulary notebook. The number in parentheses indicates the paragraph in this reading selection where the word appears.

1. individualism (1), individualistic (1), individual (2), individuality (10)
2. culture (1)
3. environment (3)
4. elements (4)
5. conflict (11)

The second list is of Academic Words that are new in this reading selection. Add these words to your vocabulary notebook. The number in parentheses indicates the paragraph in this reading selection where the word appears.

1. rely (1), reliance (3), relying (6)
2. surveys (2)
3. emphasis (2)
4. survive (3)
5. community (5)
6. adults (7)
7. achieve (8)
8. role (9)
9. images (11)
10. contradictions (11)
11. majority (12), major (12)
12. dramatic (12)
13. media (13)
14. corporations (13)
15. uniformity (13)
16. core (13)

EXERCISE 10

Learning Academic Words

Do the following activities to learn these words:

1. Record the words you are learning on tape or as audio files. Or ask a native speaker to record the words for you.
2. Pause after you say each word (five seconds or so).
3. Play the recording to yourself whenever you have some spare time (for example, when you are driving in the car).
4. Repeat the word after the recording, and say the definition. This way you will get used to the spoken form of the word as well as the written form.

EXERCISE 11

Practicing with Verbs Followed by Prepositions

In English, there are some verbs that must be followed by particular prepositions. Find the verbs listed here in the reading selection. After the verb, write the preposition that goes with it. Create an original sentence with the verb and preposition. The first one has been done as an example.

1. (paragraph 1) rely on

   I rely on my parents to help me.

2. (paragraph 2) depend

   American doesn't like depends the other

3. (paragraph 3) cut

   I've cut off the meat esily

4. (paragraph 3) survive

They will survive to the storms

5. (paragraph 5) put

I gonna put the table

6. (paragraph 6) look

_____

7. (paragraph 6) relying

I don't relying

8. (paragraph 9) linked

_____

9. (paragraph 9) comes

_When he comes, he will ____

DISCUSSION ACTIVITIES

Form a group of three or four students. Review the rules for group work your class created in the activity on page 10. Choose one or more of the following activities to discuss or work on with your group members. Make sure that each person in your group has a chance to talk. One student in your group should take notes on the discussion. Choose one student from your group to summarize the discussion.

1. How old were you when you left your parents' home? What do you think is the perfect age for children to leave their parents' home? Explain your answer.

2. Think about the following categories. Find examples of individualism in American popular culture in each area. Share your examples with your classmates.
   a. Newspaper and magazine advertisements
   b. TV advertisements
   c. American music
   d. American movies

3. Make a list of typical American behaviors that are individualistic. Make another list of typical American behaviors that show they are influenced by groups. (Use the accompanying chart to help you set up your list.) Discuss the lists with your group members. Does American behavior show more group or individual influence?

Individualistic	Influenced by Groups

READING-RESPONSE JOURNAL

Choose one of the following topics, and write about it in your reading journal.

1. How can this reading selection be linked to Reading 1? What ideas are similar in each reading selection? What ideas are different?

2. What do you find contradictory in this reading? It may contradict something else the writer says or a reading in another text or in another class. It may also contradict common sense or your experience or expectations. Explain the contradictions and what you think about the ideas associated with them.

WRITING TOPICS

Choose one of the following topics, and write a composition.

1. Many immigrants to the United States feel compelled to adapt to their new country. Sometimes this adaptation means losing previously held values and adopting new ones. In your opinion, should immigrants give up their native values and try to be more like Americans? Or is it more important to maintain the values of one's cultural heritage? For you personally, which American values are the most difficult to understand or accept?

2. Describe a Hollywood movie you've seen in which rugged individualism is an important trait of the main character.

3. Read Duc-Huy Tran Nguyen's composition "Keeping to the Tradition" in *Student Impressions*. Nguyen discusses how his culture differs from American culture on the value of individualism. Write a composition identifying reasons why some cultures prefer to emphasize the welfare of the group over the rights of the individual.

STUDENT IMPRESSIONS

Duc-Huy Tran Nguyen immigrated to the United States from Vietnam. He describes how he was first exposed to the American value of individualism. He also describes the struggle that Vietnamese people face as they try to hold on to their traditional values in the United States.

Keeping to the Tradition
by Duc-Huy Tran Nguyen

On November 27, 2002, my parents and I got off an airplane that had crossed the Pacific Ocean for thousands of miles to arrive at Los Angeles International Airport. Not long after, I saw two of my uncles standing and waving to us while my aunt was holding her camera tight and taking pictures of us. We were filled with so many feelings of happiness and amazement. We were so elated because we had been separated for twelve years. Out of nowhere came the voice of my anxiety: "Would we really get help from the members of my extended family when we began our new lives in the United States?" It had been echoing in my mind when I was on board the plane, and now it showed up again. I wasn't worried about my family's decision to emigrate to the United States until I heard the story of my father's best friend. It turned my eager anticipation to dreaded anxiety.

The day before my family left our beloved country, one of my father's best friends, who has lived in America for eight years, came to visit my father unannounced. This was the first time he visited his motherland since he emigrated. The conversation between him and my father was full of smiles and joy. My father told him about our going to the United States. Sitting next to my father, I expected to see his face become as joyful as ours. But instead, his eyes turned sad and his face numb, which signified to me there could be something very upsetting he would tell us.

His brother, who has lived in the United States for a long time, sponsored his family to emigrate there. Having promised financial support, his brother treated his family well for just a month and a half. Thereafter, the brother told his family to move out of his house. Dumbfounded, my father's friend asked his brother why he had to leave. His brother explained little except, "That's the American way."

Having limited English, they could survive only by getting jobs at the bottom of society. Nevertheless, that dismal destiny couldn't defeat his family's steady conviction of a better life. His wife and he worked hard as well as went to school regularly and diligently. Also, he encouraged his lovely and obedient children to study well at school. "My children didn't let me down," he said with his face less stressed and his voice happier.

His story finally came to a happy ending. His family is now living a stable life. His children have achieved and succeeded in pursuing their own goals. But for him, he thinks he has lost rather than gained—the emotional fraternal tie between his brother and him has been irretrievably loosened.

I made the crucial decision to emigrate to the United States, so I really prepared myself for living in the different world of culture here. I heard that Americans do like living independently and they do expect their children to leave their nest when they reach the age of eighteen. But I've never heard of Americans behaving like this brother did.

We all know that the most important requirement for immigration approval to the United States is having a sponsor. However, not all immigrants can find one, especially a family. Luckily, an American who is my aunt's friend agreed to become my family's sponsor, even though he didn't know what we were like. I'm truly thankful for his generous deed, and that's why I think most Americans are nice and supportive.

I was so stunned when I heard his story. I couldn't believe it was true. In our culture, siblings and relatives help and protect one another in time of need. When I was a child, I remember hearing the proverb "The stronger leaves protect the weaker ones" from my grandmother and mother. Even that kind of deed, I remember, was taught in elementary school. Thus this tradition has been absorbed and has penetrated in our bloodstream. I'm forever proud of that good tradition, and I believe Vietnamese are also proud of it.

Nevertheless, things went against my father's friend that way. They're brothers who were born and raised in Vietnamese culture and society. With that background, they should have supported each other. His brother's behavior goes against the humanitarianism of which we have been proud.

How could he easily forget the basic lesson of compassion and humanitarianism that he was obviously taught at school when he was a child? What would be the reason for the transformation of his nature? Would it be because the practical and materialistic life has ruled over the value of family in his heart? The more I blamed his brother's bad behavior, the more seriously I thought whether it would happen to my own family.

Now I have lived in the United States for nearly one year. I am happy to report that my anxiety has gone away, for my family is still living with my grandmother, my aunt, and my uncles under the same roof. How lucky my family is not to suffer the frustrating experience my father's friend did. For most Vietnamese who live in America, I really don't know if they still keep that good custom, but at least it's alive in our extended family. I believe that custom may contribute to the diversity of ethnic customs in the United States and one day it might not only be treasured by Vietnamese but also by the world.

Personal Impressions

READING 3

Prereading

Before you read, discuss the following questions with your classmates.

1. What kinds of things do Americans do to show that they value individualism?

2. This reading selection is about a man named John Muir. He had an important and lasting effect on changing how people think and act. Do you know of other people who have had a lasting effect on how people think or act?

3. John Muir is known as a famous naturalist. What is a naturalist? What do naturalists do?

Predicting

Before you read, do the following activities. They will help you predict what the reading selection will be about.

1. Look at the photo of John Muir on page 23. What kind of man do you think he is? Explain your answer.

2. Look at the specialized vocabulary in the next section. What kinds of words are there? What do you think this reading selection will be about?

Previewing Specialized Vocabulary

Listed below are some of the specialized words that you will find in this reading selection. Knowing and understanding these words will help you understand the reading selection.

- Review the definitions of these words.
- Identify which of these words, if any, you already know.
- Try to paraphrase the meaning of each word.
- Underline these words in the reading selection.

naturalist (*n.*)—a person who studies nature (paragraph 1)

Sierra Club (*prop. n.*)—a club whose main goal is to protect the natural environment (paragraph 1)

wanderlust (*n.*)—a very strong impulse to travel (paragraph 4)

Isthmus of Panama (*prop. n.*)—the narrow strip of land between the Atlantic and Pacific Oceans at Panama (paragraph 5)

Sierra Nevada (*prop. n.*)—the group of mountains that go through the state of California (paragraph 9)

Yosemite Valley (*prop. n.*)—a valley of east-central California along the Merced River (paragraph 9)

glacier (*n.*)—a huge mass of ice slowly flowing over a landmass, formed from compacted snow (paragraph 10)

pine cabin (*n.*)—a small, roughly built house made from pine logs; a cottage (paragraph 10)

Glacier Bay (*prop. n.*)—a narrow inlet of the Pacific Ocean in southeastern Alaska northwest of Juneau, surrounded by towering mountain peaks with spectacular glaciers tumbling into the bay (paragraph 10)

meadow (*n.*)—a tract of grassland, either in its natural state or used as pasture (paragraph 13)

Petrified Forest (*prop. n.*)—a section of the Painted Desert in eastern Arizona reserved as a national park, named for its fossilized trees (paragraph 13)

reservoir (*n.*)—a natural or artificial pond or lake used for the storage and regulation of water (paragraph 16)

John Muir and Conflicting American Values

▲ John Muir

1   John Muir was a farmer, inventor, naturalist, explorer, writer, and founder of the Sierra Club. He was born on April 21, 1838, in Dunbar, Scotland. Until the age of eleven, he attended school in Scotland. In 1849, the Muir family immigrated to the United States, settling in Wisconsin. The story of John Muir's life illustrates the American value of individualism. At the same time, it reflects a rejection of the American values of control over environment and materialism. A study of Muir's life shows how some American values can come into conflict.

2   Muir's father was harsh[5] and worked his family very hard. Whenever they were allowed a short period away from the hard farm work, Muir and his younger brother would roam[6] the fields and woods. John became a loving observer of the natural world. He also became an inventor, a carver[7] of curious but practical mechanisms in wood. He made clocks that kept accurate time and created a wondrous device that tipped him out of bed before dawn.

3   In 1860, Muir took his inventions to the state fair at Madison, where he won several prizes. Also that year, he entered the University of Wisconsin. He made fine grades, but after three years, he left Madison to travel to Canada. He worked at several odd jobs on his way through the yet unspoiled[8] land.

4   In 1867, while working at a carriage parts shop in Indianapolis, Muir suffered a blinding eye injury that would change his life. When he regained his sight one month

---

[5]**harsh** (*adj.*) — strict, severe
[6]**to roam** (*v.*) — to move about without purpose or plan
[7]**carver** (*n.*) — a person who cuts or shapes things from wood using a knife
[8]**unspoiled** (*adj.*) — in a natural state

later, he had a new outlook on life. Muir was so thankful that he could see again that he resolved to use his restored eyesight to study the variety of the natural world. This began his years of wanderlust. He walked a thousand miles, from Indianapolis to the Gulf of Mexico in Florida. He wasn't exactly sure of his route. His only plan was to go by "the wildest, leafiest, and least trodden[9] way." He walked twenty miles a day and stayed nights with whoever would take him in. If he couldn't find someone to stay with, he would sleep outdoors under the stars.

5   From Florida he sailed to Cuba. Later he took a ship to Panama, where he crossed the Isthmus and sailed up the West Coast of the United States. He landed in San Francisco in March 1868. From that moment on, though he would travel around the world, California became his home.

6   As soon as he arrived in San Francisco, he asked a man, "What is the nearest way out of town?"

7   "But where do you want to go?" asked the man.

8   "To any place that is wild," Muir replied.

9   So on April 1, 1868, Muir set out on foot for the Yosemite Valley. California's Sierra Nevada and Yosemite Valley were paradise to John Muir. He walked across the San Joaquin Valley through waist-high wildflowers. He climbed into the high country abutting[10] the mountains. Later he would write, "Then it seemed to me the Sierra should be called not the Nevada[11], or Snowy Range, but the Range of Light. . . . [It is]

▲ Yosemite National Park

[9]**trodden** (*adj.*) — walked on
[10]**to abut** (*v.*) — to border on, to touch
[11]***Nevada*** means "snowy" in Spanish.

the most divinely beautiful of all the mountain chains I have ever seen." Through that first summer he worked herding[12] sheep and eventually made his home in Yosemite.

10   Muir preferred to work at manual jobs in the Yosemite Valley. Although it was hard work, he had plenty of time to explore the beautiful natural environment that surrounded him. By 1871, he had found active glaciers in the Sierra. He began to be known throughout the country. Famous men of the time, including Ralph Waldo Emerson, made their way to the door of his pine cabin.

11   Beginning in 1874, Muir wrote a series of articles titled "Studies in the Sierra." This launched[13] his successful career as a writer. He left the mountains and lived awhile in Oakland, California. From there he took many trips into the wilderness. Included in these was his first trip to Alaska in 1879. There he first saw Glacier Bay. In 1880, he married Louie Wanda Strentzel and moved from Oakland to nearby Martinez, California. John and Louie had two daughters, Wanda and Helen. Family life caused him to settle down. Muir went into partnership with his father-in-law and managed the family fruit ranch with great success. But ten years as a rancher did not quell[14] Muir's wanderlust. His travels took him to Alaska, Australia, South America, Africa, Europe, China, Japan, and of course, again and again to his beloved Sierra Nevada.

12   In later years, he turned more seriously to writing. He recounted his travels in three hundred articles and ten major books. In his writings, he expounded[15] his naturalist philosophy. He encouraged everyone to "climb the mountains and get their good tidings[16]." Muir's love of the high country gave his writing a spiritual quality. His readers, whether presidents, congressmen, or plain folks, were inspired[17] and often moved to action by the enthusiasm[18] of Muir's own unbounded[19] love of nature.

13   Muir wrote a series of articles appearing in *Century* magazine. These articles drew attention to the devastation[20] of mountain meadows and forests by sheep and cattle. Muir became good friends with Robert Underwood Johnson, the associate editor of *Century*. With Johnson's help, Muir worked to stop the destruction caused by sheep and cattle. In 1890, due in large part to the efforts of Muir and Johnson, an act of Congress created Yosemite National Park. Muir was also personally involved in the creation of other national parks, including Sequoia, Mount Rainier, Petrified Forest, and Grand Canyon. Muir is often called the "father of our national park system."

14   Johnson and others suggested to Muir that an association be formed to protect the newly created Yosemite National Park. In 1892, Muir and a number of his supporters founded the Sierra Club. The purpose of the Sierra Club was, in Muir's words, to "do something for the wilderness and make the mountains glad." Muir served as the club's president until his death in 1914.

15   In 1901, Muir published *Our National Parks*. This book brought him to the attention of President Theodore Roosevelt. In 1903, Roosevelt visited Muir in Yosemite.

---

[12]**to herd** (*v.*) — to gather or tend groups of animals
[13]**to launch** (*v.*) — to put into motion
[14]**to quell** (*v.*) — to stop, to put an end to
[15]**to expound** (*v.*) — to explain in detail
[16]**tidings** (*n.*) — news
[17]**to inspire** (*v.*) — to stimulate to action; to motivate
[18]**enthusiasm** (*n.*) — great excitement for or interest in a subject or cause
[19]**unbounded** (*adj.*) — having no boundaries or limits
[20]**devastation** (*n.*) — destruction

▲ President Theodore Roosevelt and John Muir

Together, beneath the trees, they laid the foundation of Roosevelt's innovative conservation programs.

16   Muir and the Sierra Club fought many battles to protect Yosemite and the Sierra Nevada. The most dramatic of these was the campaign to prevent the damming of the Hetch Hetchy Valley. Damming would provide water for San Francisco and Los Angeles. But the Hetch Hetchy Valley was within Yosemite National Park. In 1913, after years of effort, the battle was lost and the valley was doomed to become a reservoir. The following year, after a short illness, Muir died in a Los Angeles hospital.

17   John Muir was perhaps this country's most famous and influential naturalist. He taught people the importance of experiencing and protecting our natural environment. His words have changed our perception of nature. His personal involvement in the great conservation questions remains an inspiration for environmental activists everywhere.

READING SKILLS

EXERCISE 12   **Supporting the Main Idea with Examples**

This reading selection has three main ideas:

1. Muir values individualism.

2. Muir doesn't value materialism.

3. Muir doesn't value control over the environment.

There are several examples in the reading selection to support these ideas. Review the reading selection. Find examples that support each of the main ideas. Using highlighting pens in three different colors, mark the examples that support the main ideas.

EXERCISE 13   **Comprehension Questions**

Answer the following questions using information from the reading selection.

1. What was John Muir's life like when he was a boy? What kinds of things did he like to do?

2. Do you think Muir was happy at the University of Wisconsin? Why or why not?

3. How was Muir's life changed in 1867?

4. How do you think the man reacted when John Muir said that he wanted to go to "any place that is wild"? Why would the man react that way?

5. What did Muir like about the California countryside he walked through?

6. Why did Muir prefer to work at manual jobs?

7. How did family life change Muir?

8. How have Muir's ideas influenced the way people think about nature in the United States?

9. What will Muir be remembered for?

VOCABULARY SKILLS

EXERCISE 14   ### Academic Word List

The following words are frequently found in academic writing. Knowing these words will help you read all kinds of academic texts. The first list is of Academic Words that you have seen earlier in this book. You can find these words again in this reading selection. Make sure these words are in your vocabulary notebook. (See page 7 for information about how to make a vocabulary notebook.) Add any new information that you learn about these words to your vocabulary notebook. The number in parentheses indicates the paragraph in this reading selection where the word appears.

1. conflict (1), conflicting (1)

2. environment (1), environmental (17)

3. individualism (1)

4. immigrated (1)

5. major (12)

6. dramatic (16)

The second list is of Academic Words that are new in this reading selection. Add these words to your vocabulary notebook. The number in parentheses indicates the paragraph in this reading selection where the word appears.

1. founder (1), founded (14), foundation (15)

2. illustrates (1)

3. rejection (1)

4. created (2), creation (13)

5. period (2)

6. mechanisms (2)

7. accurate (2)

8. device (2)

9. odd jobs (3), manual jobs (10)

10. injury (4)

11. resolved (4)

12. restored (4)

13. eventually (9)

14. series (11)

15. partnership (11)

16. philosophy (12)

17. editor (13)

18. involved (13), involvement (17)

19. published (15)

20. innovative (15)

21. perception (17)

EXERCISE 15

Learning Academic Words

Do the following activities to learn these words:

1. Using index cards or a pack of blank business cards, write the Academic Words on the cards.

2. On the back of the card, write the word in your first language or a definition of the word.

3. Practice the words. As you go through the cards, separate them into two piles: words you understand immediately and words you do not.

4. Keep going through the unlearned words until you can remember the meanings of all the words quickly.

5. Carry your cards with you. When you have a few spare minutes, run through the cards again.

EXERCISE 16

Practicing Collocations

Study these sentences from the reading selection.

1. He worked at several **odd jobs** on his way though the yet unspoiled land. (paragraph 3)

2. Muir preferred to work at **manual jobs** in the Yosemite Valley. (paragraph 10)

3. Although it was **hard work**, he had plenty of time to explore the beautiful natural environment that surrounded him. (paragraph 10)

These sentences use the nouns *jobs* or *work* with an adjective. In English, some adjectives are used with certain nouns and not with others. Study the accompanying chart. It shows adjectives that are commonly used with the word *job* and adjectives that are commonly used with the word *work* when it means a job. Which words can be used with *job* and not with *work*? Practice using the adjectives correctly by creating sentences with the adjectives and either *job* or *work*. The first one has been done for you as an example.

Words That Can Modify *Job*		Words That Can Modify *Work*
cushy	manufacturing	full-time
dream	menial	hard
evening	odd	manual
full-time	part-time	menial
good	routine	part-time
hard	teaching	routine
high-powered		unpaid
ideal		weekend

1. *He is always relaxed; he has a cushy job.*

DISCUSSION ACTIVITIES

Form a group of three or four students. Review the rules for group work your class created in the activity on page 10. Choose one or more of the following activities to work on with your group members. Create a presentation for your other classmates about what you have learned. Every person from your group should be a part of the presentation.

1. Use the Internet or other resources to find out about these other famous people who worked to preserve and understand nature. Each group should find out about a different famous naturalist. You may choose a person from the following list or another naturalist you know about. Explain what the person has done to help preserve or understand nature. Compare the life of the person you learn about to the life of John Muir. Share what you learn with your classmates.
   a. Jacques Cousteau
   b. Rachel Carson
   c. John James Audubon
   d. Robert Kennedy Jr.
   e. Chico Mendes
   f. Wangari Maathai

2. Use the Internet or other resources to find out about national parks in the United States. Each group should research a different national park. Share what you learn with your classmates.

READING-RESPONSE JOURNAL

Choose one of the following topics, and write about it in your reading journal.

1. What do you find stimulating or intriguing in this reading assignment? Summarize that portion of the selection, and explain why you find it stimulating.

2. How do you feel about nature? Do you like to spend time "in the wild," like John Muir? Or would you rather be indoors?

WRITING TOPICS

Choose one of the following topics, and write a composition.

1. Describe a place of natural beauty in your home country or a place you know well. Why do people cherish this place?

2. In 1867, Muir suffered an accident that changed his life forever. For one month, he was blind. Write about an event that changed your life. Explain how you live differently now.

INTERNET ACTIVITIES

For additional internet activities, go to **elt.thomson.com/impressions**

The American Idiom

A nation's language can tell us a lot about the values of that nation. The vocabulary people use, the way they talk, and the idiomatic expressions they create are all indications of the way people in a nation think and interact with one another. The United States inherited its principal language, English, from another country. But American English has developed unique characteristics. What do those unique characteristics tell us about American values? Chapter 2 addresses this question.

"We infer the spirit of the nation in great measure from the language, which is a sort of monument to which each individual has contributed a stone."

—Ralph Waldo Emerson, American philosopher

"The American language shows its character in a constant experimentation, a wide hospitality to novelty, and a steady reaching out for new and vivid forms."

—H. L. Mencken, American author

Overall Impressions

READING 1

Prereading

Before you read, discuss the following questions with your classmates.

1. How is American English different from British English?

2. Why do you think American and British English are different?

3. Besides American and British English, what other varieties of English are there?

Predicting

Predicting can help you understand what you read. Before you read, do the following activities. They will help you predict what the reading selection will be about.

1. Look at the titles of each section. What do you think each section will be about?

2. Look at the list of phrases in paragraph 11 and the illustration that goes with that paragraph. How are the phrases in that list related to each other?

3. Look at Chart 2.1 in paragraph 16. Do you know any other words that other languages have contributed to English? Do you know the meaning of the English words in the table?

4. Who speaks Yiddish? Where is Tagalog spoken?

Previewing Specialized Vocabulary

Listed here are some of the specialized words that you will find in this reading selection. Knowing and understanding these words will help you understand the reading selection better.

- Review the definitions of these words.
- Identify which of these words, if any, you already know.
- Try to paraphrase the meaning of each word.
- Underline the words in the reading selection.

census (*n.*)—the official count of the population, usually done by the government (paragraph 4)

Appalachian (*adj.*)—related to a mountainous area of the United States known for its distinct culture (paragraph 7)

accent (*n.*)—a particular way of speaking typical to a country or region (paragraph 7)

frontier (*n.*)—wilderness, unexplored land (paragraph 11)

poker (*n.*)—a card game that involves gambling (paragraph 11)

terminology (*n.*)—vocabulary particular to a field or place (paragraph 13)

territory (*n.*)—area or land (paragraph 15)
indigenous (*adj.*)—native to a particular area (paragraph 18)
Anglicized (*adj.*)—changed to be more like English (paragraph 18)

Languages in the United States

1   What is the official language of the United States? It's not English.

2   Many people are surprised to learn that the United States does not have an official language. Although English is the language used for government functions in the United States, the government has never given it official status.

3   The English language first arrived in North America with British colonists. From colonial times on, English has been the most widely spoken language in what is now the United States.

4   English has not been the only language used in the United States, however. Immigrants to the country have brought their native languages. Since the nineteenth century, non-English-speaking communities have established businesses, schools, and newspapers in many languages. These languages have included German, French, Italian, Czech, Polish, Chinese, Yiddish, Korean, Vietnamese, and Spanish. According to the 2000 census, 82 percent of Americans use English as their primary language at home. Another 11 percent use Spanish as their primary language. Dozens of other languages are spoken in homes across the United States.

American English

5   Is American English different from British English? The English of the United States has its roots in the language as spoken in England. American and British English are generally mutually intelligible, but there are some differences in pronunciation, spelling, vocabulary, and grammar. Occasionally, these differences can cause misunderstandings. Some people say that the United States and the United Kingdom are "two countries divided by a common language."

6   In the United States, written English is fairly uniform across the country. In speech, however, there are some variations from region to region, from class to class, and from ethnic group to ethnic group. These differences have emerged because the first settlers of North America came from distinct parts of Great Britain. People from the same region of the mother country tended to settle together in the colonies. Thus people from the east of England settled in the northern colonies, while people from the west of England settled in the southern colonies. They brought their distinctive speech patterns with them to the New World.

7   With time, new groups arrived in North America. The Scotch-Irish had a tremendous influence on the English spoken in the Appalachian Mountain region. Germans contributed to the accent and vocabulary of Pennsylvania. Scandinavians and French speakers also introduced new features to the language. Also, Africans first brought as slaves learned English and contributed many words and expressions.

8   Today, Americans can hear very noticeable differences in the native speech of Bostonians, New Yorkers, southerners, and Texans. The residents of cities such as Chicago and Philadelphia also have distinct speech patterns. You can identify the sounds of American speech by listening to recent presidents. John F. Kennedy spoke

▲ John F. Kennedy

▲ Jimmy Carter

▲ Bill Clinton

▲ George W. Bush

with a Boston accent. Jimmy Carter from Georgia and Bill Clinton from Arkansas both speak with southern accents. George W. Bush speaks with a Texas accent. The most widespread and familiar American accent is called "standard midwestern." This is the accent heard in the speech of most newscasters and radio announcers.

America's Contributions to the English Language

9   English has been spoken in North America for four hundred years.

10   During that time, the language has changed in many ways. Americans have contributed to these changes. For example, some words that are now common throughout the English-speaking world were first used in America. These words include *lengthy*, *bookstore*, and *calculate*.

11   As settlers moved west, the frontier experience brought new vocabulary to the language. For example, the favorite card game on the frontier was poker. The game's vocabulary has enriched English with many words and phrases, including these:

- You bet!
- Call someone's bluff

- The cards are stacked against me!
- Hit the jackpot
- The chips are down
- Poker face

12   Similarly, the favorite frontier drink, whiskey, led to the addition of words like *bartender*, *cocktail*, *hangover*, and *bootlegging* to the language.

13   Every aspect of frontier life added words to English. Cowboys used new words like *maverick* and *rustler*. They used new phrases, too: *bite the dust* and *hot under the collar* are examples of cowboy phrases that are now commonly used in English. American railroad terminology came into the language as well. Today, most people don't realize that the words *sidetracked* and *streamline* refer to trains. Likewise, the phrases *to be in the clear*, *to make the grade*, and *end of the line* started as railroad terms.

14   In 1849, gold was discovered in the mountains of California. Hundreds of thousands of people hurried west, hoping to get rich. The California Gold Rush added new phrases to the English language, such as *lucky strike*, *to stake a claim*, *to pan out*, and *bonanza*.

Other Languages' Contributions to American English

15   Spanish contributed new words to the English vocabulary. The word *bonanza* came from Spanish. As English-speaking Americans moved west across North America, they encountered Spanish speakers in the territory that belonged to Mexico (the United States acquired this territory after fighting a war with Mexico in 1846). Words like *stampede*, *ranch*, *rodeo*, and *lasso* all come from Spanish.

▲ An American cowboy

16   In fact, many of the words that Americans have added to the language actually come from other languages, such as German, Dutch, French, and Yiddish. Consider these immigrant contributions:

TABLE 2.1

English Word	Original Language
Hoodlum	German Bavarian
Scram	Yiddish
Cookie	Dutch
Chowder	French Canadian
Tycoon	Japanese
Boondocks	Tagalog
Gung ho	Chinese

17   Besides words, immigrants have added new idiomatic expressions to American English. From German come such expressions as *no way*, *let it be*, and *and*

how! Some familiar sentences are simply translations of sayings from other languages. Have you ever heard anyone say, "I need it like a hole in the head"? This expression comes from Yiddish, as does another American favorite: "Get lost!"

18   When Europeans arrived in North America, they encountered the continent's indigenous peoples. English speakers adopted American Indian words for many things, including foods, plants, animals, geographical features, and cultural artifacts. Usually, these words were "Anglicized," meaning that English speakers altered the words to make them easier for them to pronounce. *Squash, woodchuck, bayou,* and *powwow* originated as American Indian words. Many American place names also come from indigenous languages. For example, Chicago, Illinois, takes its name from different indigenous words. *Chicago* comes from an Algonquian Indian word meaning "onion field." *Illinois* was originally a French version of *Illiniwek,* the name of the native people in what is now the state of Illinois.

19   English is now one of the most widely spoken languages in the world and one of the most popular for study. Because of immigration, languages from all over the world have made major contributions to the development of English. This trend is likely to continue well into the future.

READING SKILLS

EXERCISE 1   **Finding the Main Idea**

Choose the main idea for each section.

1. What is the main idea of the first section (paragraphs 1–4), "Languages in the United States"?
   a. English is not the official language of the United States.
   b. British Colonists first brought English to the United States.
   c. English is not the only language in the United States.
   d. Most people in the United States speak English or Spanish.

2. What is the main idea of the second section (paragraphs 5–8), "American English"?
   a. The United States and the United Kingdom are two countries divided by a common language.
   b. American presidents, like American people, speak with different accents.
   c. Scotch-Irish, Germans, and African Americans had the greatest influence on American English.
   d. Written English is similar in the United States, but many people speak with different accents.

3. What is the main idea of the third section (paragraphs 9–13), "America's Contributions to the English Language"?
   a. American frontier life added many new words and phrases to English.
   b. English has been spoken in North America for over four hundred years.

    c. Cowboys added more words and phrases than gold miners.

    d. Some American English words, such as *lengthy, bookstore,* and *calculate,* are now also used in British English.

4. What is the main idea of the fourth section (paragraphs 15–19), "Other Languages' Contributions to American English"?

    a. Spanish was the first language to contribute words to American English.

    b. Other languages have contributed words and idioms to American English.

    c. Most of the Native American words in English are the names of places.

    d. Americans tend to Anglicize words contributed by other languages.

EXERCISE **2**   **Reviewing for Details**

One of the purposes of this reading is to give examples of words that make American English different. Work with a partner. Review the reading selection. Make a list of all the words and idioms in American English mentioned in this reading selection. Discuss the meaning of the words with your partner.

VOCABULARY SKILLS

EXERCISE **3**   **Academic Word List**

The following words are frequently found in academic texts. Knowing these words will help you read all kinds of academic texts. The first list is of Academic Words that you have seen earlier in this book. You can find these words again in this reading selection. Make sure these words are in your vocabulary notebook. (See page 7 for information about how to make a vocabulary notebook.) Add any new information that you have learned about these words to your vocabulary notebook. The number in parentheses indicates the paragraph in this reading selection where the word appears.

1. immigrants (4)	**3.** uniform (6)	**5.** major (19)
2. communities (4)	**4.** cultural (18)	

The second list is of Academic Words that are new in this reading selection. Add these words to your vocabulary notebook. The number in parentheses indicates the paragraph in this reading selection where the word appears.

1. functions (2)	**4.** primary (4)	**7.** region (6)
2. status (2)	**5.** mutually (5)	**8.** emerged (6)
3. established (4)	**6.** variations (6)	

9. ethnic (6), ethnicities

10. distinct (6), distinctive (6)

11. contributed (7), contributions (16), contribute (14)

12. features (7)

13. identify (8)

14. widespread (8)

15. likewise (13)

16. aspect (13)

17. grade (13)

18. encountered (15, 18)

19. acquired (15)

20. trend (19)

EXERCISE 4

Practicing Academic Words

Write the Academic Word that goes with each definition.

1. _____Structure_____ rank, position
2. _____establish_____ set up, started, created
3. _____Primary_____ most important, major
4. _____likewise_____ equally
5. _____Variation_____ differences, alternatives
6. _____Region_____ area, district
7. _____Emerge_____ came out, appeared
8. _____Aspect_____ characteristics, traits
9. _____identified_____ name, classify
10. _____Encounter_____ met, came across
11. _____Acquired_____ got, obtained
12. _____trend_____ movement, tendency

EXERCISE 5

Acquiring Dictionary Skills

Some English words have several meanings. You can use a dictionary to find out the specific meaning of a word in a sentence.

Example:

> **function** (fungk′ shən) *n.* 1. A specific occupation or role. 2. An official ceremony. 3. A term in mathematics.

Use a dictionary to find the meanings of each of the following words. Look the words up in the dictionary. Find the definition that matches how the word is used in the sentence. The first one has been done for you as an example.

1. Although English is the language used for government **functions** in the United States, the government has never given it official status.

   function: *A specific occupation or role*

2. In the United States, written English is fairly **uniform** across the country.

uniform: _____

3. Every **aspect** of frontier life added words to English.

aspect: _____

4. Likewise, the phrases *to be in the clear, to make the* **grade***,* and *end of the line* started as railroad terms.

grade: _____

5. Americans of all ethnicities have made **major** contributions to the development of the language.

major: _____

EXERCISE 6

Expanding Dictionary Skills

American English often uses words from other languages. We call these "borrowed" words. In a dictionary, you can find the meaning and the pronunciation of words. A dictionary such as the *American Heritage Dictionary* will also tell you which language the English word came from. Here is an example.

> **boondocks** (boon′doks) *pl. n. Slang* 1. Wild and dense jungle. 2. Rural country. [From Tagalog *bundok*, mountain.]

From this dictionary entry, we can see that *boondocks* comes from Tagalog, the main language spoken in the Philippines.

Form groups of three or four students. Divide the following list of words among the different groups. Look the words up in the dictionary. Write the words' definitions and what language they are borrowed from. The first one has been done for you as an example.

Word	Meaning	Language of Origin
boondocks	*jungle; rural country*	*Tagalog*
arsenal		
bandana		
barbecue		
boss		
bum		
canyon		
casino		
cinnamon		

(continued)

Word	Meaning	Language of Origin
coffee	*Arabe.*	*Arabe.*
cookie	*Cookid.*	
cotton	*Arabe.*	
ghetto	*A part of the city where people from*	*Italian*
hazard	*a particular race or group especially*	
iceberg	*people who are poor, live separately*	
	from the rest of the people in the city	
ketchup		
khaki	*– Indi*	
mattress		
pajamas		
robot	*A machine that can move and do some of the*	
sandal	*work of a person as is usually controled by*	
scarlet	*computer. (Czech) Robota work.*	
	– A bright red color – French. Latin	
semester		
seminar		
shampoo		
shawl	*= Piece of soft word, usually in a*	
	square or irregular shape –	
skate		
smorgasbord	*:A large variety of foods which are put*	
	on a long table so that people can	
sofa	*serve themselves*	
syrup	*(A large variety of different things*	
tea	*Arabe.*	
tulip	*– Turkish.*	
tycoon	*:someone who is successful in business*	*Japanes*
umbrella	*or industry and has a lot money*	
	and power	
vampire		
zigzag		

Handwritten margin notes (left side): *Dutch, Malay, Arabe, Greek, German, Persia, Dutch, Turkish, Dutch, Italian, Vampire, German.*

DISCUSSION ACTIVITIES

Form a group of three or four students. Choose one or more of the following activities to discuss or work on with your group members. Review the rules for group work your class created in the exercise on page 10. Make sure that each person in your group has a chance to talk. One student in your group should take notes on the discussion. Choose one student from your group to summarize the discussion.

1. Do you think Americans should make English the official language of the United States? Why or why not? List five reasons to support each side of this issue.

2. Why do you think the frontier had such a great influence on American English? With your group, brainstorm a list of reasons. Share your reasons with your classmates.

3. Are there words that other languages have borrowed from English? Make a list of English words that are found in other languages. Use a dictionary to help you find borrowed words.

fazard.

READING-RESPONSE JOURNAL

The best readers think about what they read. One way to think about what you have read is to write about it. Choose one of the following topics, and write about it in your reading journal.

1. What do you find practical or useful in this reading assignment? It might be useful in your daily life now, in your professional life now or in the future, or in your academic research as you prepare to write a paper. What specifically is useful, and how can it be used?

2. What do you find interesting in this reading assignment? Summarize the point of interest, and then explain why you find it interesting.

WRITING TOPICS

Choose one of the following topics, and write about it.

1. Does your native language borrow words from other languages? What words have been borrowed? Why do you think languages borrow words from each other? (See "Student Impressions" on page 42 for one student's response to this question.)

2. Idiomatic phrases are expressions that cannot be understood from the meanings of the individual words that make up the expression. For example, "She was the apple of his eye" is an idiomatic expression. Choose one of the following idiomatic expressions. Explain what it means, and give examples of when it might be used by a native speaker of English.

   a. break the bank

   b. can't hold a candle to (someone)

   c. cut my teeth on (something)

   d. a white-knuckle ride

3. New words are constantly added to American English. Here are some examples of words that have recently been added to American English. Choose one of the words, write a definition of the word, and explain how it might be used by a native speaker of English.

   a. metrosexual

   b. blog

   c. flash mob

STUDENT IMPRESSIONS

Eunice Kamau came to the United States from Keyna. She is a college student in Georgia. In her studies, she has learned about the many languages that have contributed to American English. This reminds her of the many influences on her native language, Swahili. For her English class, she wrote an essay about these different influences.

The Swahili Language
by Eunice W. Kamau

The Swahili language is basically of Bantu (African) origin. It is believed that the language was introduced to the coast of East Africa in the second century C.E. History states that Swahili originated with Arab and Persian merchants who visited the East African coast and used to speak with the natives in their local language. They intermarried with them and then came up with a new language called Swahili. It has borrowed words from Arabic, probably as a result of the Swahili people using the Qur'an (Koran), written in Arabic, for the spiritual guidance of Muslims.

It is an undeniable truth that Arab and Persian cultures had the greatest influence on the Swahili language. For example, *chai* ("tea"), *achari* ("pickle"), and *serikali* ("government") are words borrowed from Persian, bearing testimony to the older connections with Persian merchants.

The Swahili language also absorbed words from the Portuguese during the time that Portugal controlled the East African coastal towns from 1500 to 1700. Some examples are *leso* ("handkerchief"), *meza* ("table"), and *pesa* ("peso, money"). Swahili also borrowed some words from English during the colonial era, for example *baiskeli* ("bicycle"), *basi* ("bus"), *penseli* ("pencil"), and *mashine* ("machine").

Trade and migration from the East African coast during the nineteenth century helped spread the language to the interior of East, Central, and South Africa. Swahili is the most widely spoken language on the African continent, and some nations have declared it the national language. Swahili is also making its presence felt in the art world. It is the language of songs, drama, movies, and television programs. The lyrics of the song "Liberian Girl" by Michael Jackson has Swahili phrases: *Nakupenda pia, nakutaka pia, Mpenzi we* ("I love you, and I want you, my dear").

It is well known that any language, as it grows and expands its territories, will absorb some vocabulary from other languages along the way, and Swahili has been able to achieve popularity because of its association with other languages.

In-Depth Impressions

READING 2

Prereading

Before you read, discuss these questions with your classmates.

1. Have you noticed a difference between the way Americans speak English and how they write it? Give examples of some differences.

2. Have you noticed that Americans have different accents? What are some of the accents that Americans have?

3. Do you ever have difficulty understanding how some Americans talk? Share a time when you had difficulty understanding an American accent.

4. What do you know about the history of African Americans in the United States?

Predicting

Predicting can help you understand what you read. Before you read, do the following activities. They will help you predict what the reading selection will be about.

1. Look at the title of this selection. What do you think the title means?

2. Look at the words and definitions on page 45. Have you heard any of the words before? When did you hear them? What do you think this reading selection is going to be about?

3. Look at Diagram 2.1 on page 46. What kind of information does it tell you? How do you think it will help you understand the reading selection?

Previewing Specialized Vocabulary

Listed here are some of the specialized words that you will find in this reading selection. Knowing and understanding these words will help you understand the reading selection.

- Review the definitions of these words.
- Identify which of these words, if any, you already know.
- Try to paraphrase the meaning of each word.
- Underline these words in the reading selection.

dialect (*n.*)—a variety of language of a particular region or social group (paragraph 1)

linguist (*n.*)—a person who studies languages (paragraph 2)

vernacular (*adj.*)—related to the way people talk in everyday situations, usually specific to one region (paragraph 3)

plantation (*n.*)—a large farm found mostly in the American South before the U.S. Civil War when most of the farm laborers were slaves imported from Africa (paragraph 4)

pidgin (*n.*)—a simplified language that usually has a mixture of words from two or more different languages (paragraph 4)

tote (*v.*)—to carry (paragraph 7)

banjo (*n.*)—a musical instrument with five strings (paragraph 7)

bogus (*adj.*)—false, not real (paragraph 7)

impediment (*n.*)—an obstacle; something that stops or slows the progress of a process (paragraph 8)

socioeconomic mobility (*n. ph.*)—the ability to move from one social and economic group to another, as when a lower-class person becomes a middle- or upper-class person (paragraph 8)

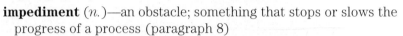

African American Vernacular English

1   American English is not all the same. It is a broad category that includes the different types of English spoken in the United States. There are several distinct dialects, including Northern, Midland, Southern, and Appalachian.

2   What is a dialect? Some people think that dialects are inferior or substandard variations of a given language. But this is not the case. According to linguists, a dialect is simply a regional or social variety of a language. Usually, dialects have differences in pronunciation, grammar, or vocabulary. Any suggestion of a dialect's inferiority has more to do with social perceptions than linguistic reality.

3   One of the most interesting American dialects is associated with an ethnic group: African Americans. Linguists use the term African American Vernacular English (AAVE) to describe the kind of English spoken in some African American communities. Some scholars also use the term Ebonics to identify this dialect.

4   The history of AAVE begins with the transatlantic slave trade. Africans were taken from their homelands across the ocean to the Americas. The slaves spoke many different languages. On the slave plantations, slaves were forced to live and work together. Most did not speak the same language, but they had to communicate. They learned some English from the slave traders and plantation owners. They used what they learned to speak to one another in a kind of pidgin English. Over several generations, some of the characteristics of this pidgin language became fixed, and a new dialect of English emerged.

▲ The mistreatment of a slave in the nineteenth century

5   Many features of this dialect come from African languages. Some grammatical structures can be traced to West African languages. For example, many verbs in AAVE are used in ways verbs are used in certain African languages. For example, one feature of AAVE is the use of *be* to indicate habitual performance. Standard English usage does not readily indicate this tense through verb forms. When a speaker of AAVE says, "He be playing guitar," this means "He plays guitar often or all the time." In AAVE, the phrase refers to regular, ongoing action.

6   Many people who are not familiar with AAVE may think that a sentence like "He be playing guitar" is not grammatical. They think it is an indication of ignorance of the rules of English. But that is not the case. Linguists note that the grammar of AAVE has a system of regular rules. As with any dialect, it takes time to understand and appreciate these rules.

7   AAVE is not only a language for African Americans. It has influenced standard English, especially in vocabulary. For example, many words in standard English came from AAVE. *Tote, banjo*, and *bogus* are examples. Some linguists believe that *OK* may have an African origin. Furthermore, AAVE has introduced new slang words to English speakers. Popular African American musical styles, such as jazz and rap, have added to the American vocabulary. Here are some examples:

> *hip*: wise, sophisticated
> *hype*: persuasive talk
> *sharp*: neat, smart
> *square*: a person who is not sophisticated
> *have a ball*: to enjoy yourself
> *in the groove*: perfect
> *out of this world*: exceptional

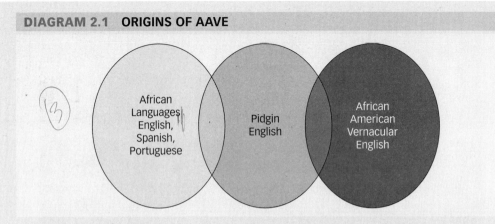

DIAGRAM 2.1   ORIGINS OF AAVE

8   AAVE appears in the written works of famous African American writers such as Langston Hughes, Zora Neale Hurston, and Toni Morrison (who won the Nobel Prize). African American church ministers and entertainers also use AAVE for dramatic purposes. Nevertheless, many people—black and white—regard AAVE as a sign of poor education. Because of this, the use of AAVE can be "an impediment to socioeconomic mobility," according to linguist John Rickford, of Stanford University. In other words, African Americans who only speak AAVE can have a difficult time finding a good job. It can prevent them from holding high status in society. Many African Americans learn to change dialects. They use AAVE in informal communication with other AAVE speakers. But they switch to standard English in formal settings such as school or the workplace. This process of adapting language use to different social contexts is called *code switching.*

9   Some people criticize AAVE and consider its use controversial. However, linguists unanimously recognize it as a legitimate dialect. Rickford puts it this way: "This dynamic, distinctive variety—thoroughly intertwined with African American history and linked in many ways with African American literature, education, and social life—is one of the most extensively studied and discussed varieties of American English, and it will probably continue to be so for many years to come."

READING SKILLS

EXERCISE 7   **Reviewing for Details**

Look back at the reading, and answer the questions.

1. According to the reading selection, what are some other dialects of American English?

2. What is another name for AAVE?

3. What effect did the slave trade have on AAVE?

4. How did slaves communicate when they first arrived in the United States?

5. What is one feature of AAVE that came from West African languages?

6. How do linguists know that AAVE is a dialect of English and not just bad grammar?

7. List five vocabulary words that AAVE has introduced to American English.

8. How do you know that Toni Morrison is a good writer?

9. What does "AAVE may be an impediment to socioeconomic mobility" mean?

10. What is the process of adapting language use to different social contexts called?

11. According to John Rickford, why is AAVE important?

EXERCISE 8   **Reading a Diagram**

Diagrams and other graphic organizers can help us understand difficult concepts in a text. Use Diagram 2.1 to do the following activities.

1. What information is the graphic organizer trying to show?

2. Why do the circles overlap?

3. Work with a partner. Reread the text that explains the graphic. Without looking at the text, explain to your partner how AAVE developed. Your partner should add any detail that you missed.

VOCABULARY SKILLS

EXERCISE 9   **Academic Word List**

The following words are frequently found in academic writing. Knowing these words will help you read all kinds of academic texts. The first list is of Academic Words that you have seen earlier in this book. You can find these words again in this reading selection. Make sure these words are in your vocabulary notebook. (See page 7 for information about how to make a vocabulary notebook.) Add any new information that you learn about these words to your vocabulary notebook. The number in parentheses indicates the paragraph in this reading selection where the word appears.

   1. ethnic (3)   **2.** generations (4)

The second list is of Academic Words that are new in this reading selection. Add these words to your vocabulary notebook. The number in parentheses indicates the paragraph in this reading selection where the word appears.

1. category (1)   **3.** traced (5)   **5.** ignorance (6)

2. structures (5)   **4.** indicate (5)   **6.** appreciate (6)

EXERCISE **10**   **Practicing Academic Words**

Use a definition and synonyms to make a visual representation of a word. Compare your "picture" of the word with a partner. Here is an example:

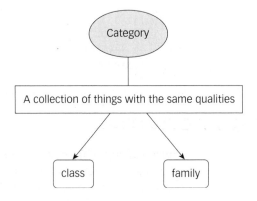

Your Visual Representation

EXERCISE **11**   **Acronyms**

An acronym is a word made from the initial letters of a name. In this reading selection, AAVE means African American Vernacular English. Here are some other acronyms. Use a dictionary to find out the meaning and pronunciation of each acronym. Note that some acronyms are pronounced letter by letter, and others are pronounced as words.

Acronym	Meaning
AIDS	
ASAP	
FBI	
FIFA	*Federal Integration Fotball Aovaut*
GMT	*Greeu Mint time*
IOC	*Internotino Olmpicos Comuut*
IRS	*Internal Renevcu Servicci*
NAACP	*NATIONAL ASOCFATION FOR ADVANCES OF COLOR POEPLE*
NGO	
RADAR	*Radio detectuipuy au ru Euginr*
SCUBA	*Self contaue underwater*
UNICEF	*Ouitel Intennatiou childreu*

DISCUSSION ACTIVITIES

Form a group of three or four students. Review the rules for group work your class created in the activity on page 10. Use the Internet or other sources to find out additional information about some of the topics mentioned in this reading selection. Share what you have learned with your classmates. Be sure to cite the sources you used to find additional information.

1. Find information about the writers mentioned in this article— Langston Hughes, Zora Neale Hurston, Toni Morrison—or another famous African American author who uses AAVE in his or her writing. Find a passage that shows how the author writes in AAVE.

2. Find five additional words that AAVE has added to American English. Explain what each word means and how it is used in mainstream American culture.

3. Besides AAVE, what are some other regional dialects used by Americans? Choose one of these dialects, and study how it is different. What words does it use that are different? Does it use different grammar? Do the speakers of this dialect pronounce words differently?

READING-RESPONSE JOURNAL

Choose one of the following topics, and write about it in your journal.

1. One purpose of this reading selection is to convince or persuade the reader that AAVE is an important dialect of American English. How can you tell what purpose the author has in mind? Does the author use good arguments to support the ideas in the reading? Do you agree with the author?

2. What do you find unclear in this reading assignment? Summarize the section you find unclear, explain what you think it means, and discuss why you're still uncertain.

WRITING TOPICS

Choose one of the following topics, and write a composition.

1. Choose one of the research topics you did as a group discussion activity. Expand your thoughts on the topic by writing a short three-to five-page research paper on the topic. Be sure to site the sources you used to find additional information.

2. Everyone practices code switching every day. You talk differently to your teachers than you do with your friends and parents. Write an essay explaining how you use code switching. In your introductory paragraph, define what code switching is. In each of your body paragraphs, explain how you talk differently with different groups of people. Give specific examples of what you might say when talking to each group. Explain what might happen if you used the wrong "code" with one group.

3. Although linguists agree that AAVE is a dialect of English, many African Americans and other Americans consider it "bad English." What is your opinion? Should African Americans be discouraged from speaking AAVE? Defend your answer with specific examples.

4. John Rickford says that "AAVE may be an impediment to socioeconomic mobility." Do you believe that people discriminate against others because of their accent or the way they talk? Support your opinion with specific examples. The examples can be from English or another language you know about.

Personal Impressions

READING 3

Prereading

Before you read, discuss the following questions with your classmates.

1. What is a poem? Do you like to read poetry?

2. Have you ever heard of Walt Whitman? What do you know about him?

3. This reading selection ends with part of a poem by Whitman about different jobs of common people. Here are the jobs he mentions: mechanic, carpenter, mason, boatman, deckhand, shoemaker, hatter, woodcutter, ploughboy, mother, sewing girl, washing girl. How many of these jobs have you heard of? Which jobs are new to you? Can you guess what those people do in their jobs?

Predicting

Before you read, do the following activities. They will help you predict what the reading selection will be about.

1. Look at the photo of Walt Whitman. What kind of person do you think he is?

2. In paragraph 2, we learn that Walt Whitman was born in 1819. What do you think life was like then?

Previewing Specialized Vocabulary

Listed here are some of the specialized words that you will find in this reading selection. Knowing and understanding these words will help you understand the reading selection better.

- Review the definitions of these words.
- Identify which of these words, if any, you already know.
- Try to paraphrase the meaning of each word.
- Underline these words in the reading selection.

journalist (*n.*)—a writer or reporter for a newspaper or magazine (paragraph 2)

rhyme (*n.*)—words or poetry that have the same ending sound, as for example, *hat, cat,* and *that* (paragraph 3)

meter (*n.*)—the measured rhythm of words in poetry (paragraph 3)

discouraged (*adj.*)—no longer having confidence (paragraph 4)

wit and wisdom (*n. ph.*)—intelligence and knowledge (paragraph 4)

cathedral (*n.*)—a large church (paragraph 6)

democratic (*adj.*)—allowing all people to participate in the political system and granting them broad rights and freedoms (paragraph 6)

TEXT

idealism (*n.*)—belief in high standards or principles (paragraph 6)

inspired (*adj.*)—having exciting special qualities that encourage others (paragraph 7)

carols (*n.*)—songs (paragraph 8)

blithe (*adj.*)—happy, not worried (paragraph 8)

intermission (*n.*)—a break (paragraph 8)

robust (*adj.*)—strong and healthy (paragraph 8)

melodious (*adj.*)—musical, pleasing to the ear (paragraph 8)

Walt Whitman: A Man of Words

▲ Walt Whitman

1   The United States has produced several renowned poets, including Emily Dickinson, Robert Frost, and Langston Hughes. Of all the great American poets, however, Walt Whitman is considered the most representative of the American spirit.

2   Walt Whitman was born in 1819. He grew up in Brooklyn, New York. After dropping out of school at the age of twelve, he worked as a printer in Brooklyn and Manhattan. Later he became a journalist and wrote articles for newspapers in New York and New Orleans. As a reporter, he walked all over New York City and Long Island, observing people at work and at play. He wrote poems about what he saw and heard.

3   The poems that Whitman wrote were very different from the kind of poetry that was popular at the time. He did not use rhyme or traditional meters. Instead, Whitman tried to write poetry that used the language he heard people speaking on the streets—the actual language of real people. Because his poetry was unique, Whitman had a hard time finding a publisher. In 1855, he used his own money to publish the first edition of *Leaves of Grass*.

4   Today, *Leaves of Grass* is regarded as the most important book ever written by an American poet. But at the time it was published, almost no one liked it. Whitman was not discouraged. He continued to write poems. By 1860, a publisher in Boston wanted to print a new and expanded edition of *Leaves of Grass*. A famous American philosopher, Ralph Waldo Emerson, read the book and said it was "an extraordinary piece of wit and wisdom." Whitman's poetry began to receive greater recognition.

5   For the rest of his life, Whitman added more and more poems to each new edition of *Leaves of Grass*. These poems, like Whitman's earlier poems, reflect on the American experience. For example, during the Civil War (1861–1865), Whitman worked as a volunteer in the hospitals of Washington, D.C. He visited wounded soldiers, trying to cheer them up and help them recover from their wounds. Hearing their stories, Whitman wrote a series of poems about the war. These poems describe the suffering and bitterness that soldiers experience in war.

6   For the last twenty years of his life, Whitman lived in Camden, New Jersey. Several more editions of *Leaves of Grass* were published, each with new poems. The last edition appeared in 1892, the year of Whitman's death. Whitman said that his book was like a cathedral long under construction, growing larger and more elaborate with the years. In this "cathedral," he wanted to capture the spirit of the American people. He wrote about the work of common people. More important, he discovered a new kind of poetry in the way common Americans spoke. In his poems, Whitman tried to give a voice to the democratic experiment taking place in the United States. He succeeded in creating a literature to match the size, the potential, and the idealism of the nation in its first century of existence. In *Leaves of Grass*, he spoke directly to the citizens of the United States, calling on them to be generous, ambitious, and devoted to the ideals of political liberty.

7   Whitman's influence on American poetry has been enormous. His success in using unrhymed free verse inspired many poets to write in a similar fashion. Walt Whitman invigorated the English language, finding poetic expression in the speech of everyday Americans. For this reason, he is revered as the father of American poetry.

8   These lines are taken from *Leaves of Grass*. In them, the poet describes working people and their fondness for singing.

> I hear America singing, the varied carols I hear;
>
> Those of mechanics, each one singing his, as it should be, blithe and strong;
>
> The carpenter singing his, as he measures his plank or beam,
>
> The mason singing his, as he makes ready for work, or leaves off work;
>
> The boatman singing what belongs to him in his boat, the deckhand singing on the steamboat deck;
>
> The shoemaker singing as he sits on his bench, the hatter singing as he stands;
>
> The wood-cutter's song, the ploughboy's, on his way in the morning, or at the noon intermission, or at sundown;
>
> The delicious singing of the mother, or of the young wife at work, or of the girl sewing;
>
> The day what belongs to the day—at night, the party of young fellows, robust, friendly,
>
> Singing with open mouths, their strong melodious songs.

READING SKILLS

EXERCISE 12

Finding the Main Idea

Match the main idea with the paragraph.

a. paragraph 2   c. paragraph 4   e. paragraph 6

b. paragraph 3   d. paragraph 5   f. paragraph 7

___C___ **1.** After Emerson commented on *Leaves of Grass*, Whitman's poetry became popular.

___F___ **2.** Whitman is considered the father of American poetry.

___D___ **3.** One of the subjects Whitman wrote about was the Civil War.

___E___ **4.** Whitman's poems were very different from other poetry at the time, so they were not very popular at first.

___A___ **5.** Although he dropped out of school, Whitman was a successful writer.

___B___ **6.** In *Leaves of Grass*, Whitman tells the story of everyday American people in poetry.

EXERCISE 13

Reviewing for Details

Look back at the reading, and answer the questions.

1. Who is another famous American poet? -Dickinson

2. What was Whitman's first job? Printer

3. Why did Whitman have a difficult time finding a publisher for his poetry? his poetry was unique.

4. How did people first react to the poetry in *Leaves of Grass*?

5. Where did Whitman work during the Civil War? hospital Washita,

6. What two things happened in 1892?

EXERCISE 14

Reading Poetry

A poet uses words to create images or pictures that illustrate an idea. In this poem, Whitman creates images of people who take pride and satisfaction in their work to illustrate the idea that even common and physical jobs can make people happy. For example, in line 3, Whitman speaks of "The carpenter singing his [song], as he measures his plank or beam." The image of the singing carpenter gives us an image of a person who is happy with his job.

List four other examples of images that Whitman uses to illustrate his idea.

1. _____

2. _____

3. _____

4. _____

VOCABULARY SKILLS

EXERCISE 15   **Academic Word List**

The following words are frequently found in academic writing. Knowing these words will help you read all kinds of academic texts. The first list is of Academic Words that you have seen earlier in this book. You can find these words again in this reading selection. Make sure these words are in your vocabulary notebook. (See page 7 for information about how to make a vocabulary notebook.) Add any new information that you learn about these words to your vocabulary notebook. The number in parentheses indicates the paragraph in this reading selection where the word appears.

1. traditional (3)   **3.** philosopher (4)   **5.** similar (7)

2. publisher (3),   **4.** creating (6)
    publish (3),
    published (4)

The second list is of Academic Words that are new in this reading selection. Add these words to your vocabulary notebook. The number in parentheses indicates the paragraph in this reading selection where the word appears.

1. unique (3)   **5.** recover (5)   **9.** devoted (6)

2. expanded (4)   **6.** series (5)   **10.** enormous (7)

3. edition (4)   **7.** potential (6)   **11.** varied (8)

4. volunteer (5)   **8.** construction (6)

EXERCISE 16   **Learning Academic Words**

Do the following activities to learn these words.

1. Circle the words you already know. Use a dictionary to find the meanings of the words you do not know.

2. Find the word on this list with a meaning that is the opposite of an Academic Word. Write the Academic Word next to its opposite.

a. deteriorate _____

b. common _____

c. alike _____

d. innovative _____

e. brief _____

f. tiny _____

g. uncommitted _____

h. conscript _____

i. destruction _____

j. destroying _____

EXERCISE 17   **Recognizing Nouns in the Same Word Family**

Word families are groups of related words. Many words have more than one noun form. Use the dictionary as needed to fill in the different forms of the noun that is a name of a person or job. The first one has been done for you as an example.

Nouns	Person or Job
poetry, poem	*poet*
journalism	
report	
observation	
philosophy	
idealism, ideal	
citizenship	
masonry	
carpentry	
shoe	
hat	

DISCUSSION ACTIVITIES

Form a group of three or four students. Review the rules for group work your class created in the activity on page 10. Choose one or more of the following activities to discuss or work on with your group members.

Make sure that each person in your group has a chance to talk. One student in your group should take notes on the discussion. Choose one student from your group to summarize the discussion.

1. If Walt Whitman were writing about the songs of the working people in your city or town today, what jobs or occupations might he write about? With your group members, make a list of songs.

2. From the list of jobs or occupations in Whitman's poem, what can you infer about male and female roles in the 1800s? Have those roles changed today? In what ways are they similar or different?

3. Do you have a favorite poem (in English or your first language)? Share your favorite poem with your group members. Explain what the poem means.

READING-RESPONSE JOURNAL

Choose one of the following topics, and write about it in your reading journal.

1. What event in Whitman's life was the most interesting to you? Why did you choose that event?

2. The main idea of Whitman's poem is that even common and physical jobs can make people happy. Do you agree with this idea? Are there any downsides to common and physical jobs?

3. Is the story of Whitman's life similar to that of any other famous person you know? Who? How are their lives similar?

WRITING TOPICS

Choose one of the following topics, and write a composition.

1. Walt Whitman got the ideas for his writing by observing people working and playing. Go to a busy place like a construction site, mall, park, or city street where you can observe people working or playing. Listen to what people say, and watch carefully what they are doing. Describe what you see and what people are doing and saying.

2. Whitman was not successful as a poet at first, but he was not discouraged. Describe a person who overcame obstacles and ultimately succeeded.

3. Poetry is important to people in many different cultures. What do poets contribute to a nation or culture's sense of identity?

INTERNET ACTIVITIES

For additional internet activities, go to **elt.thomson.com/impressions**

Immigrant Impressions

homework 61-65. Next class.

The United States has often been referred to as a nation of immigrants. Except for Native Americans, all people in the United States are immigrants or descendants of immigrants. In the first section of this chapter, you will learn a little about the history of immigration in the United States and some of the struggles of modern immigrants. The second section discusses some of the difficulties that adolescent immigrants experience. The final reading selection tells the story of Leonid Yelin, a recent immigrant to the United States.

> **"**We must remember we are all descendents of immigrants.**"**
>
> —Franklin D. Roosevelt, U.S. president

Overall Impressions

READING 1

Prereading

Before you read, discuss the following questions with your classmates.

1. Why do people immigrate to the United States?

2. What are some of the challenges that people who immigrate face?

3. What are some contributions that immigrants have made to the United States?

4. What do you know about the history of immigration in the United States?

Predicting

Predicting can help you understand what you read. Before you read, do the following activities. They will help you predict what the reading selection will be about.

1. Look at the photos. What do you think this reading selection will be about?

2. Look at Graph 3.1. What information can you learn from the graph?

3. In what years did the greatest number of immigrants come to the United States?

4. What could have caused the immigration rate to fall in the 1930s?

Previewing Specialized Vocabulary

Listed here are some of the specialized words that you will find in this reading selection. Knowing and understanding these words will help you understand the reading selection better.

- Review the definitions of these words.
- Identify which of these words, if any, you already know.
- Try to paraphrase the meaning of each word.
- Underline these words in the reading selection.

pluralistic (*adj.*)—having many parts (paragraph 1)

Protestant, Catholic (*adj.*)—related to the two different branches of the Christian religion (paragraph 4)

persecution (*n.*)—the act of oppressing or discriminating against people because of their race, religion, or ethnic background (paragraph 4)

influx (*n.*)—arrival in large numbers (paragraph 6)

menial jobs (*n. ph.*)—jobs as servants or unskilled workers (paragraph 11)

quota (*n.*)—a specific percentage or part of the whole promised to or reserved for a particular group (paragraph 15)

inflow (*n.*)—arrival (paragraph 16)

Immigration in the United States

1   The United States is a nation of immigrants. Immigrants make America a more pluralistic and diverse society. In addition, they contribute to the culture of the United States. They affect U.S. values in important ways. Immigrants have always helped the American economy grow. To some extent, the American economy depends on laborers from other countries. Even though the United States needs their cheap labor, immigrants have not always been accepted. There have been cultural clashes[1] between Americans and immigrant groups throughout U.S. history. Sometimes these clashes have been violent. The experiences of several ethnic groups in the United States illustrate this point.

Conflicts

2   Before the 1840s, about 60,000 immigrants arrived in the United States each year. During the 1840s and 1850s, the number of people coming to the United States increased dramatically. Over three million Irish and Germans crossed the Atlantic for America at this time.

GRAPH 3.1   **IMMIGRATION TO THE UNITED STATES, 1820–2010**

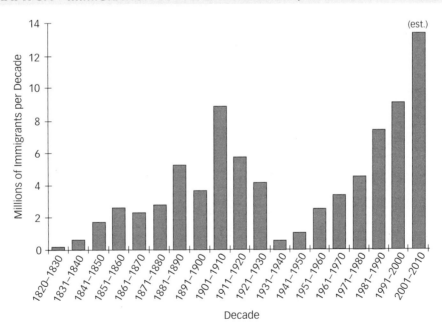

3   Why did they leave their homelands? Immigrants came to the United States for many reasons. Europe was becoming crowded. America was inviting and spacious[2].

---

[1]**clashes** (*n.*) — conflicts or fights
[2]**spacious** (*adj.*) — large, roomy

It was the "land of freedom and opportunity." Immigrants believed they would find religious freedom and better jobs. They also came because taxes were lower in the United States. Another reason was that many European countries required men to serve in the military. The United States did not have laws that required military service.

Irish Immigrants

4   The reality that the Irish found in America did not match their hopes. Most Irish immigrants lived in extreme poverty. Most settled in the slums[3] of Boston and New York. Some in the Protestant majority considered the Catholic newcomers a social problem. These newcomers had different customs. Occasionally, religious clashes led to violence. The Irish could find work only in low-paying jobs. Irish women worked as kitchen maids. Irish men took dangerous jobs at low wages. Many found no work at all just because they were Irish. Employers posted signs that read "No Irish Need Apply" in store windows and on factory gates. Despite this open persecution, with time the Irish were successful. They established businesses and bought property. Eventually, they became a powerful force in the political life of Boston, New York, and Chicago.

German Immigrants

5   Millions of Germans also came to America in the middle part of the 1800s. In general, these immigrants came with more money and training than the Irish. They were able to buy land in the Midwest. Many became farmers in states such as Ohio and Wisconsin.

6   The Germans had a notable influence on American culture and customs. For example, the Christmas tree was a tradition brought by German immigrants. Another example is in the area of public education. They established the concept of the *kindergarten*, literally the "children's garden." This is how kindergarten became a part of the modern educational system. The popularity of beer in America is another result of the influx of Germans.

▲ Levi Strauss

7   Some of these immigrants made lasting contributions to American culture. For example, a Jewish tailor from Germany named Levi Strauss migrated to the United States in 1847. He traveled to California at the time of the Gold Rush (1849). Levi designed sturdy overalls[4] out of heavy cloth. The overalls quickly became popular among gold miners. They were so popular that he opened a factory in San Francisco. His overalls, known as blue jeans or Levi's, made him a wealthy and famous man.

8   Germans made many contributions to America. However, some people were distrustful of the Germans.

---

[3]**slums** (*n.*) — the crowded and poor parts of a city
[4]**overalls** (*n.*) — loose-fitting pants with shoulder straps usually made out of strong fabric

They established communities separate from other Americans. They kept their native language and culture. They formed their own militia and fire companies. They sponsored German schools. At these schools, the children learned German instead of English. There were German-language newspapers. Because the Germans remained separate, other Americans resented them.

Chinese Immigrants

9   The next wave of new immigration came after the Civil War. Nearly twelve million people arrived between 1870 and 1900. Most of these newcomers were German, Irish, or English. At the same time, many Chinese came to the West Coast. From 1849 to 1882, about 300,000 Chinese moved to the United States. However in 1882, a new federal law stopped most Chinese from coming into the country.

▲ An anti-Chinese poster from the 1800s

10   By 1880, about 75,000 Chinese, mostly men, lived in California. They represented about 9 percent of the state's population. Life was hard for Chinese immigrants. They worked in the goldfields They also helped build railroads. Others worked at menial jobs. They were cooks, laundrymen, or servants. They faced many hardships, including violence.

11   Americans distrusted the Chinese more than other immigrants. In 1882, the U.S. Congress passed a law against Chinese immigrants, the Chinese Exclusion Act. This *Troebles* law kept nearly all Chinese from entering the country. For the first time, the U.S. government restricted immigration, singling out people from one country—China. This reflected open prejudice against the Chinese. They were singled out because they looked different from the German and Irish immigrants. The Chinese Exclusion Act remained in effect for nearly sixty years.

12   Like other immigrant groups, the Chinese in time overcame hardships and discrimination. Like the Germans, they built separate communities. "Chinatowns" emerged in railroad towns, farming villages, and cities. In these communities, the Chinese ran their own small businesses. They formed social organizations and started schools.

The Next Wave

13   The flow of immigrants continued from 1880 to 1920. There were more new arrivals every year. Between 1900 and 1914, between 500,000 and 1.2 million people came each year. The year of the biggest influx was 1907, when almost 1.3 million people moved to the United States. Earlier most immigrants came from Western Europe. After 1880, there was a new wave of immigrants, this time from southern and eastern Europe. The largest groups in this new wave were Italians and Poles.

14   Two million Polish immigrants came between 1870 and 1914. Most of the Poles headed for industrial cities such as Buffalo, Pittsburgh, Detroit, and especially Chicago. They worked as unskilled laborers. They took jobs in coal mines, meatpacking[5] factories, textile and steel mills[6], oil refineries[7], and sewing factories.

▲ Immigrant children at school

Restricting Immigration

15   The Chinese Exclusion Act of 1882 was the first of several immigration laws. In the 1920s, new laws slowed immigration. The National Origins Act of 1924 created quotas. The quotas regulated how many immigrants from various countries could enter. The quotas for some countries were very strict. For example, the law allowed only 2,700 Russians to enter each year. The quotas also limited the number of Poles and Italians. They controlled how many people could come from southern and eastern Europe. Many of these people were Catholic. Protestant Americans did not welcome Catholic immigrants. Moreover, the law did not let any Asians enter. President Calvin Coolidge summed up the people's feelings at the time. He said, "America must be kept American." In a short time, the number of immigrants fell from 1.2 million to 280,000 a year. The quota system remained for over forty years. Even today, parts of it are still in effect.

---

[5]**meatpacking** (*n.*) — the job of cutting up an animal so it can be sold as meat
[6]**textile and steel mills** (*n.*) — factories where cloth and steel are made, respectively
[7]**oil refineries** (*n.*) — a place where oil is treated to get rid of the impurities

The Latest Wave

16   At the end of the twentieth century, there was a new surge[8] in immigration. Millions of people moved to the United States in the 1980s and 1990s. This was the heaviest inflow in American history. Unlike previous waves, however, these immigrants came mostly from Latin America, Africa, and Asia. Though they are from different parts of the world, the latest immigrants have come to America for much the same reasons as other immigrants. They are looking for economic opportunity or political freedom. And their experience is almost the same as previous immigrants. They find work in dangerous, low-paying jobs. They face discrimination, hostility[9], and anti-immigrant laws. It is difficult for them to gain the American dream. Yet they have contributed to the nation's rich and diverse culture.

17   New immigrants to the United States have always tended to settle in specific regions. In the past fifty years, most immigrants have gone to California, New York, Texas, Florida, New Jersey, and Illinois. In fact, one-third of all U.S. immigrants go to California. Immigrants now represent 25 percent of the population of California.

The Future of Immigration

18   But will new immigrants find opportunity in America? Some analysts say that new immigrants will have limited economic success. The world economy has changed over the past thirty years. Changes in technology and globalization have eliminated many well-paying skilled industrial jobs. More manufacturing jobs are moving outside of the United States. These changes could mean that immigrant families will have fewer chances for economic success. Will the new economy change immigration in the future? How will immigrants adapt? Will Americans welcome immigrants in the future? The answers to these questions are uncertain.

---

[8]**surge** (*n.*) — a rush or flood
[9]**hostility** (*n.*) — unfriendliness

READING SKILLS

EXERCISE 1   ### Finding the Main Idea

Review the reading selection. Choose the main idea of each section.

1. What is the main idea of paragraph 1?
   a. The United States is a nation of immigrants and a pluralistic and diverse society.
   b. Even though immigrants are important to the United States, they have not always been welcomed by Americans.

2. What is the main idea of paragraph 2?
   a. Before 1840, immigration did not have an effect on the United States.
   b. After 1840, immigration increased dramatically.

3. What is the main idea of paragraph 3?

   a. Immigrants came to the United States for several reasons.

   b. Only Europeans had to serve in the military.

4. What is the main idea of paragraph 4?

   a. The biggest problem for Irish immigrants was caused by religious differences between Catholics and Protestants.

   b. Life was difficult for the Irish in the United States, but eventually they became successful.

5. What is the main idea of paragraph 5?

   a. The Germans were generally more successful than the Irish because they had money and education.

   b. Many Germans became farmers in the Midwest.

6. What is the main idea of paragraph 6?

   a. Germans influenced American culture.

   b. German traditions have more influence than Irish traditions on Americans today.

7. What is the main idea of paragraph 7?

   a. Levi Strauss is an example of a successful German immigrant.

   b. Levi's jeans are named after Levi Strauss, a tailor who emigrated from Germany.

8. What is the main idea of paragraph 8?

   a. Americans were suspicious of Germans because they lived in separate communities.

   b. It is not a good idea for immigrants to keep their own language and culture because it makes Americans suspicious.

9. What is the main idea of paragraph 9?

   a. There were more German, English, and Irish immigrants than Chinese immigrants.

   b. Many Chinese immigrated to the United States beginning in 1870.

10. What is the main idea of paragraph 10?

   a. Life was hard for the Chinese in the United States.

   b. The Chinese were mostly men.

11. What is the main idea of paragraph 11?

   a. The Chinese Exclusion Act discriminated against the Chinese.

   b. The Chinese Exclusion Act was in effect for almost sixty years.

12. What is the main idea of paragraph 12?

   a. The Chinese were successful in their separate communities.

   b. The Chinese Exclusion Act said that the Chinese had to live in "Chinatowns."

13. What is the main idea of paragraph 13?

    a. Immigrants continued to come to the United States between 1880 and 1920.

    b. Between 1880 and 1920, most immigrants came from southern and eastern Europe.

14. What is the main idea of paragraph 14?

    a. Poles preferred to live in cities.

    b. The Poles mostly worked as unskilled laborers.

15. What is the main idea of paragraph 15?

    a. In the 1920s, the United States made laws to restrict immigration.

    b. The quota system remained for over forty years.

16. What is the main idea of paragraph 16?

    a. In the 1980s and 1990s, most immigrants came from Asia and Latin America for the same reasons as earlier immigrants.

    b. Attaining the American dream is difficult.

17. What is the main idea of paragraph 17?

    a. New immigrants tend to settle in specific areas.

    b. California is a popular place for immigrants to settle.

18. What is the main idea of paragraph 18?

    a. Future immigrants may not have the economic success of past immigrants.

    b. The world economy has changed.

EXERCISE 2

Organizing Details

One way to remember what you read is to organize the details of a reading selection. Complete the following chart with details from the reading selection. The first item has been done for you as an example.

Immigrant Group	Jobs	Hardships	Contributions to American Society
Irish	*Maids; dangerous low-paying jobs*		
Germans			
Chinese			
Southern and Eastern Europeans			

EXERCISE **3**   **Reading Graphs**

Use Graph 3.1 and the reading selection to answer the following questions.

1. What do the numbers at the left edge of the graph represent?

2. What years are covered by the graph?

3. Before 1980, what decade had the most immigrants?

4. The lowest number of immigrants came in what two decades?

5. What two decades had the greatest number of immigrants?

6. According to the reading selection, what caused the number of immigrants to decline after 1910?

7. According to the reading selection, why has the number of immigrants grown each decade since 1940?

8. Do you think the number of immigrants will increase or decrease between 2011 and 2020? Explain your answer.

VOCABULARY SKILLS

EXERCISE **4**   **Academic Word List**

The following words are frequently found in academic writing. Knowing these words will help you read all kinds of academic texts. The first list is of Academic Words that you have seen earlier in this book. You can find these words again in this reading selection. Make sure these words are in your vocabulary notebook. (See page 7 for information about how to make a vocabulary notebook.) Add any new information that you learn about these words to your vocabulary notebook. The number in parentheses indicates the paragraph in this reading selection where the word appears.

1. immigration, immigrants (1)

2. contribute (1), contributions (7), contributed (16)

3. culture, cultural (1)

4. ethnic (1)

5. illustrate (1)

6. dramatically (2)

7. majority (4)

8. established (4)

9. eventually (4)

10. tradition (6)

11. communities (8)

12. emerged (12)

13. created (15)

14. regions (17)

The second list is of Academic Words that are new in this reading selection. Add these words to your vocabulary notebook. The number in parentheses indicates the paragraph in this reading selection where the word appears.

1. diverse (1)	**8.** area (6)	**15.** summed (15)
2. economy (1), economic (16)	**9.** designed (7)	**16.** previous (16)
3. laborers, labor (1)	**10.** federal (9)	**17.** specific (17)
4. affect (1)	**11.** restricted (11), restricting (15)	**18.** analysts (18)
5. required (3)		**19.** technology (18)
6. military (3), militia (8)	**12.** discrimination (12)	**20.** globalization (18)
7. despite (4)	**13.** exclusion (15)	**21.** eliminated (18)
	14. regulated (15)	

EXERCISE 5

Learning Vocabulary Words

Do the following activities to learn these words.

- Look over the lists of Academic Words.
- Circle the words that you already know.
- Write each word you do not know on a note card. On the back of the note card, write a definition of the word or write the word in your first language.
- Use the note cards to study the words you do not know.

EXERCISE 6

Studying Word Parts

A suffix is the end part of a word. Suffixes can add meaning to words or can change the word's part of speech. The suffixes *-tion* and *-sion* can be used to change a verb to a noun. Add the suffix to each group of words in the following chart to change a verb into a noun. Write an original sentence with the noun you create. The first item has been done for you as an example.

Nouns Formed with *-tion*		Nouns Formed with *-sion*
contribute	*contribution*	comprehend
discriminate		conclude
educate		discuss
illustrate		exclude
immigrate		impress
organize		
persecute		
populate		
regulate		

1. *Immigrants make an important contribution to the United States.*

DISCUSSION ACTIVITIES

Form a group of three or four students. Review the rules for group work your class created in the activity on page 10. Choose one or more of the following questions to discuss with your group members.

1. With your group members, make a list of the advantages and disadvantages of living in a pluralistic and diverse society. Share your list with other groups.

2. Because of the changing economy, new immigrants may not be able to achieve the American dream as earlier immigrants have done. What advice would you give to someone who would like to immigrate today?

READING-RESPONSE JOURNAL

The best readers think about what they read. One way to think about what you have read is to write about it. Choose one of the following topics, and write about it in your reading journal.

1. Copy three sentences from this reading selection that give facts. Copy three sentences that you think reflect the opinion of the author and may not be true facts. Explain how you know whether these are facts or opinions.

2. Choose one of the pictures that illustrate this reading selection. Explain three things that you learned from this picture.

3. What do you find useful in this reading selection? It might be useful in your daily life now, in your professional life now or in the future, or in your academic research as you prepare to write a paper. What specifically is useful, and how can it be used?

STUDENT IMPRESSIONS

Cecelia Rivera is from Mexico. She is studying at Mount San Antonio College in California. In this essay, she writes about the difficulty in making the transition from one culture to another.

It Takes Courage!
by Cecilia Rivera

Being a foreigner in the United States is harder than it seems. It takes time and effort to become adapted to a new culture—in this case, the American culture. When I came to the United States, I left behind my family, my work, and my friends. I packed my books, my photographs, and my personal things and said goodbye to my country, Mexico. A new life was waiting for me. I was ready for the transition. Nonetheless, with the changes came the challenges. Everyday things can turn into a bother when you try to adapt to a new culture. I thought it was going to be easy to adjust to the social environment, the food, and the language. The fact is that it takes more time and courage than I had ever imagined.

When I first arrived in the United States, the weather was sunny, the temperature was mild, nature was blooming, and I could feel the fresh wind on my face. Everything was an adventure—the adventure of the new. I felt excited and eager to meet people from all over the world. Unfortunately, after some days in this country, I noticed something really strange. Nobody was interested in me; few people noticed that I was new in the country, and people who knew that I had just moved here did not notice me. How come? Isn't it weird that people don't treat you in a considerate way when you arrive in a place for the first time? It was obvious that American society was not very enthusiastic about foreigners; indeed, it is indifferent. More shocking was the indifference of the international community. For me, meeting other foreigners was a good way to discover the world. People from other countries were for me a source of culture and information, but they were too busy to share their culture. Most of them just cared about work; that was why they came here. Some of them did not even care about the traditions in their country anymore; those were no longer important in their lives. I wondered why this happened. Is it globalization? Is it because we are in California and the people just want to work and retire young? Is it the well-known individualism of the United States? Or maybe they had just become adapted.

I missed the holidays and the warm Mexican personality; I also missed the food of my country. California used to belong to Mexico, and that is evident in the name of some streets and cities. The influence in the cooking is an example too. If one of my goals was to learn as much from American and international culture as possible, I had to try the food too. Exploring Vietnamese, Chinese, Japanese, Korean, Indian, African, and American food was a delightful experience for me; nevertheless, I missed Mexican food. Since I did not have a stove or enough time to prepare a meal, I had resigned myself to eating Mexican fast food. This was a terrible experience. American fast food was a bad copy of real Mexican food. When I told that to people from other countries, they expressed the same opinion about their food in American restaurants. That meant that all that delightful international food that I had been eating was not as good as the original. Maybe this is not a big deal for most people, but an idea was growing in me: in my search to adapt, I asked myself, "What should I do to become adapted to American culture without losing the essence of my cultural identity?" Maybe I was taking this situation too seriously. I had better be more easygoing if I wanted to enjoy my experience in the United States.

When I came to the United States, my primary goal was to learn English; consequently, I had to make friends in English. That is difficult in California, where a large percentage of the people speak Spanish. Therefore, I decided to make friends by getting involved in all kinds of activities: salsa dancing, photography, and art classes. Then I got a part in a theater performance, that was really helpful in making me feel more confident about my speaking skills. Every activity that required me to speak in English was a good opportunity to learn and make friends. I have to accept that after one year living in this country, my English is still very poor, and sometimes it is frustrating because I can't express my ideas in a deep way. Understanding what people say is not a big problem. When I don't understand them, I just ask them to repeat slowly. Sometimes they have to explain the meanings of words. My frustration comes when I want to express my feelings and ideas; I can't find the words that fully express my thinking. It is in those moments that I lose patience. My feeling is that I don't belong in this place, that I have to go back to my country, where I can say everything in the way I like, with the words I want. What keeps me here? What should I do? Should I run away to my country?

When you move to another country, change is necessary, but traditions are important too. If we don't learn what the past tells us, how can we know who we are or who we want to be? And how can we face the present in the best way? If we don't know our purpose when we make decisions, it is difficult to be strong enough to change what we need to change in order to confront new circumstances. At the same time, we must keep our essence— the legacy that builds our identity and makes us unique humans being capable of seeing the world in so many different ways. Maybe *purpose* is the key word. After living a period in loneliness, confusion, and frustration, I asked myself, "What should I do?" "What keeps me here?" I thought about my purpose. My purpose is my future. It is my source of strength to enjoy life even if I am away from what I love most. I am still looking for a better way to become adapted to this country. It is clear that being a foreigner has not been easy for me; however, this experience has let me meet cherished people who have helped me and taught me important life lessons.

WRITING TOPIC

This writing exercise will help you with essay writing. This model of organizing an essay is very common in U.S. colleges and universities. The basic pattern of *introduction, body, conclusion* is favored by U.S. professors. If you organize your writing according to this pattern, you will improve your chances of getting good grades at universities in the United States. Here is the topic:

Cecilia Rivera writes that she came to the United States to learn English. She found out, however, that learning English in the United States is more difficult than she had thought. She encountered obstacles. What obstacles have you encountered while you have been learning English? Write an essay that explains your experiences.

There are many good ways to organize and present an essay on this topic. Here is one model you might use:

Introduction. In your first paragraph, tell your readers why you want to learn English. Give some background details about your education. When and where did you start learning English? How long have you been studying English? Conclude the introductory paragraph with a sentence that identifies the two most important obstacles that have made learning English difficult for you. This sentence, called a *thesis statement,* tells the reader what you intend to discuss in the body of the essay.

Body paragraph 1. Write about the first obstacle that made it difficult to learn English. Give specific examples of mistakes you made. Tell about specific times when you faced this obstacle.

Body paragraph 2. Write about the second obstacle that you identified in the thesis statement. Again, give specific examples of when you faced this obstacle.

Conclusion. In your final paragraph, tell your readers how you plan to overcome those obstacles. In your experience, what has been the best way for you to learn English?

In-Depth Impressions

READING 2

Prereading

Before you read, discuss the following questions with your classmates.

1. Do you think it is easier to immigrate as an adult or a child? Why?

2. Have you ever tried to translate for people who speak different languages? What are some of the problems of being a translator?

3. Immigrants may have different values than people in their new country. What happens when the values of different cultures come into conflict with each other?

Predicting

Before you read, do the following activities. They will help you predict what the reading selection will be about.

1. Look at the title of this reading selection. What do you think "Generation 1.5" means?

2. Read the **bold** headings. Discuss with your classmates what you think each section is about.

Previewing Specialized Vocabulary

Listed here are some of the specialized words that you will find in this reading selection. Knowing and understanding these words will help you understand the reading selection.

- Review the definitions of these words.
- Identify which of these words, if any, you already know.
- Try to paraphrase the meaning of each word.
- Underline these words in the reading selection.

adolescents (*n.*)—young people between thirteen and seventeen years old (paragraph 3)

refugees (*n.*)—people who have to leave their homeland, usually because of war (paragraph 3)

language brokering (*n. ph.*)—serving as a translator, usually without formal training, for people who do not speak the same language (paragraph 8)

stereotype (*n.*)—an overly simple idea or image of a person (paragraph 12)

newcomer schools (*n. ph.*)—special schools that help immigrant children adjust to the United States (paragraph 14)

segregation (*n.*)—the practice of separating people by class or race (paragraph 14)

self-esteem (*n.*)—pride in oneself; self-respect (paragraph 14)

Who Belongs to "Generation 1.5"?

1   Traditionally, we classify immigrants according to when their families arrive in the United States. Newly arrived immigrants are called the *first generation*. The children of first-generation immigrants are called the *second generation*. Their grandchildren are called the *third generation*, and so on.

2   These categories are helpful. However, it is not easy to put immigrants into categories. Not all first-generation immigrants have the same experiences. They come from many different countries and have different backgrounds. One important difference among first-generation immigrants is their age when they arrive. Scholars now recognize that the experiences of immigrants can vary a lot, depending on how old they are when they arrive in the United States.

3   Some immigrants arrive as adults. They have already completed their education in their home country. Many others, however, arrive in the United States as children or adolescents. They come to the United States with their parents or sometimes as orphaned refugees. These younger immigrants began their lives and their educations in their native countries. Like adult immigrants, they have life experiences that include two or more cultures and languages. However, they are different from adult immigrants because they start their education in one place and complete it in a new country and a new language. These young people are different in many ways from first-generation immigrants who arrive as adults. They are also very different from second-generation immigrants. They are in between.

4   Scholars in immigration studies, education, and other fields call this in-between group "Generation 1.5." The characteristics and educational needs of the members of Generation 1.5 are somewhere between first-generation adults and the second-generation children of immigrants. "Generation 1.5" has become a popular term because it captures the in-between position of young people who do not fit in traditional categories.

5   It is important to understand how many young people fall into this category. Currently, about one million immigrants arrive in the United States each year. More than 30 percent of these immigrants are children under the age of eighteen. This is the largest wave of new immigrant children in U.S. history.

Challenges of Generation 1.5 Students

6   Most people believe that immigrant children adapt easily to their new country. However, research suggests that they often have many difficulties. For example, immigrant children often feel upset or depressed. They must leave behind their

familiar homeland, family, and friends. For these children, the adjustment is difficult. They may have difficulties even after many years in the United States.

7   Immigrant children generally have more family responsibilities than U.S.-born children. Many immigrant parents work long hours in multiple jobs. They must do this in order to make enough money to support their family in the United States. Therefore, many immigrant children must take care of themselves. Sometimes they also have to act as parents for younger brothers and sisters. Also, immigrant children are often under pressure to begin work or leave school at an early age so that they can help support their families.

Language Brokering

8   Another responsibility of Generation 1.5 is *language brokering*. A language broker translates for people who do not speak the same language. However, a language broker usually does not have any formal training. Many immigrant children act as language brokers for their parents. They translate in stores or government offices.

They may even translate at the doctor's office. For example, the Vietnamese American writer lê thi diem thúy[10] recalls her experience as a language broker. She became "the representative head of my family" because she could speak English. She took on the role of an adult in her family. She ended up "navigating[11] my family through the perils[12] of daily life, from finding milk at the grocery store to locating the correct room to enter at the social services building or the hospital."

Value Conflicts

9   Perhaps the greatest difficulty facing immigrant children is the conflict of values. Immigrant children suffer stress in adapting to American culture. The values of American culture and their native culture can be in conflict. However, immigrant children usually adopt American values more quickly than their parents.

10   The children learn that new values can differ from their parents' values. This can cause conflict with their parents. For example, immigrant children who dress and act like American children may seem disrespectful. In order to adapt, immigrant children go between two drastically[13] different social worlds. They must fit in at home and in American culture. They experience conflicting values on a daily basis.

11   An eloquent writer, lê thi diem thúy tells of the conflict she experienced growing up in California after coming from Vietnam. She "acquired a taste for dill pickles [and] macaroni and cheese, and was an expert at the Hula-Hoop and roller

---

[10]***lê thi diem thúy*** (*prop. n.*) — This Vietnamese writer prefers to spell her name without capital letters. Her name is pronounced "lay tee yim twee."

[11]**to navigate** (*v.*) — to find one's way

[12]**perils** (*n.*) — dangers

[13]**drastically** (*adv.*) — significantly and dramatically

skating backwards." But her parents kept their Vietnamese traditions. They ate foods such as ginger-fried fish, *lichee* nuts, and noodle soup, which reminded her of "an entire history I thought I'd thrown overboard like so much useless luggage adrift[14] in the watery vaults of the Pacific." Her family home seemed like "a distant outpost[15] of Vietnam." When she left the house, her parents and Vietnam seemed far away. She summarized her in-between status this way: "I had been rowing back and forth, in a relentless[16] manner, between two banks of a wide river."

Discrimination

12   As lê thi diem thúy's experience suggests, immigrant children have a difficult task. They must develop a home-culture identity and a U.S.-culture identity at the same time. Besides family pressures, immigrant children often experience discrimination. In schools, some teachers may treat students like they are not intelligent because they do not speak English. In contrast, other teachers may have expectations that are very high. This is often the case with Asian immigrants, who must live up to the stereotype of "model minority."

13   Generation 1.5 students face other problems at school. Students often show prejudice against Generation 1.5 students. For example, some students, especially native-born Americans, may see Generation 1.5 students as "foreigners."

Even students from their own culture may show prejudice. They see Generation 1.5 students as backward. They sometimes call them F.O.B. ("fresh off the boat") to suggest how backward they are. On the other hand, recently arrived immigrants may think Generation 1.5 students are "too Americanized." Other minority groups such as African Americans may see Generation 1.5 students as competing with them for better jobs and education.

Newcomer Schools

14   Immigrant children confront many more disruptions in their education. They must learn to adapt to the English-dominant culture and to a new schooling system. In some school systems, services for immigrant students may be limited. In other places, there are programs like the "newcomer school." This is a special school where immigrant children learn how to adjust to the United States and learn basic English. The value of newcomer schools has been debated. Critics argue that such schools cause more problems than they solve. They may enhance

---

[14]**adrift** (*adj.*) — floating freely
[15]**outpost** (*n.*) — a small settlement away from large cities
[16]**relentless** (*adj.*) — without stopping, persistent

segregation. They add more disruption to students' schooling and delay students' entry into mainstream school life. Advocates claim, by contrast, that such schools and programs provide a "foot up" for newcomers. They help the children with the adaptation process and affirm the value of home cultures. They also help newcomers build confidence and self-esteem.

estimar

READING SKILLS

EXERCISE 7   ## Finding the Main Idea

Match the main idea with each section of the reading selection.

a. paragraphs 1–5
b. paragraphs 6–7
c. paragraph 8
d. paragraphs 9–11
e. paragraphs 12–13
f. paragraph 14

_____ **1.** Generation 1.5 immigrants face discrimination by teachers and students in school.

_____ **2.** Generation 1.5 immigrants have problems adapting. Those problems include depression, adjustment difficulties, and more family responsibilities.

_____ **3.** Some people believe that newcomer schools help Generation 1.5 students; others believe that such schools make the transition harder.

_____ **4.** Generation 1.5 immigrants are different from first- or second-generation immigrants.

_____ **5.** When children translate for their parents, they take on adult responsibilities.

_____ **6.** When immigrant children adopt American values, it can cause problems in their families.

EXERCISE 8   ## Improving Reading Comprehension

Choose the correct answer based on the reading selection.

1. Second-generation immigrants
   a. arrive in the United States as adults.
   b. are the children of immigrants.
   c. arrive in the United States as children or adolescents.
   d. are not as important as first-generation immigrants.

2. Which is not a characteristic of Generation 1.5 immigrants?

    a. They start their education in one country and finish it in another.

    b. They are sometimes orphaned refugees.

    c. They sometimes come to the United States with their parents.

    d. They complete their education in their home country.

3. About how many Generation 1.5 immigrants arrive in the United States every year?

    a. 30,000

    b. 30 percent

    c. 300,000

    d. 1 million

4. What causes Generation 1.5 immigrants to feel upset or depressed?

    a. They leave behind their familiar homeland, family, and friends.

    b. They are in between.

    c. They are not traditional.

    d. They adapt easily to their new country.

5. Which is not a family responsibility of Generation 1.5 immigrants?

    a. They act as parents to their brothers and sisters.

    b. They go to work to help support their family.

    c. They work long hours in multiple jobs.

    d. They may act as translators for their parents.

6. How did lê thi diem thúy take on the role of an adult in her family?

    a. She regularly translated for her parents in important situations.

    b. She was the head of her family.

    c. She adopted American values.

    d. She kept Vietnamese traditions.

7. How do value conflicts make life more difficult for immigrant children?

    a. The children have to teach American values to their parents.

    b. The children must switch back and forth between American values and their parents' values.

    c. The children prefer their parents' values over American values.

    d. The children tend to be disrespectful toward their parents.

EXERCISE 9

Comprehension Questions

Answer the following questions.

1. Where are some places that children act as language brokers?

2. How does language brokering affect the traditional immigrant family structure?

3. How does lê thi diem thúy describe her feelings about being between two cultures?

4. Describe how different groups of students discriminate against Generation 1.5 students.

5. What are the advantages and disadvantages of newcomer schools?

EXERCISE 10   **Recognizing Figurative Language**

Sometimes writers use figurative language. Figurative language is used to make pictures or images in a reader's mind, often by comparing something unfamiliar to something familiar. Here are three quotations from lê thi diem thúy in this reading selection. Each uses figurative language. Reread the paragraph that contains each quote. Then explain the meaning of each quotation.

1. "navigating my family through the perils of daily life" (paragraph 8)

2. "an entire history I thought I'd thrown overboard like so much useless luggage adrift in the watery vaults of the Pacific" (paragraph 11)

3. "rowing back and forth, in a relentless manner, between two banks of a wide river" (paragraph 11)

VOCABULARY SKILLS

EXERCISE 11   **Academic Word List**

The following words are frequently found in academic writing. Knowing these words will help you read all kinds of academic texts. The first list is of Academic Words that you have seen earlier in this book. You can find these words again in this reading selection. Make sure these words are in your vocabulary notebook. (See page 7 for information about how to make a vocabulary notebook.) Add any new information that you learn about these words to your vocabulary notebook. The number in parentheses indicates the paragraph in this reading selection where the word appears.

Variar
1- Cambiar

1. traditionally (1), traditional (4), traditions (11)

2. generation (1)

3. categories (2), category (5)

4. vary (2)

5. role (8)

6. conflict (9), conflicting (10)

7. adapting (9), adapt (10), adaptation (14)

8. status (11) *- Estado*

The second list is of Academic Words that are new in this reading selection. Add these words to your vocabulary notebook. The number in parentheses indicates the paragraph in this reading selection where the word appears.

*Modification
Ajuste.*   *Resumen*

*Modificar
Ajustar
Adaptarte.*

1. depressed (6)
2. adjustment (6), adjust (14)
3. locating (8)
4. stress (9)
5. acquired (11)

6. expert (11)
7. summarized (11)
8. task (12) *Tarea*
9. intelligent (12)
10. contrast (12)

11. debated (14)
12. enhance (14) *Realzar*
13. assist (14)

EXERCISE 12

Learning Academic Words

Do the following activities to learn the Academic Words.

1. Write the words in a list on a piece of paper.

2. Study the list of words. Write a definition for the words that you already know.

3. Find the words in the reading selection. Try to guess the meaning of the words from the sentence they are in. Write definitions for the words you can guess.

4. Compare your word list with a partner's list. Use a dictionary to make corrections to your list or to find out the meaning of words you do not know.

EXERCISE 13

Recognizing Collocations

Most verbs in English go together with particular prepositions. For example, in paragraph 1, you will find this sentence:

> Traditionally, we classify immigrants by when their families <u>arrive in</u> the United States.

In English, the verb *arrive* can be followed by the prepositions *in*, *at*, and *on* but not *to*; in other words, English speakers do not say "arrive to."

Following are eight prepositions and some other verbs from the reading selection that go with one or more of those prepositions.

- Write the preposition that goes with each verb.
- Say the verbs together with the prepositions. This will help you remember which verbs and prepositions go together.

The first preposition has been filled in for you as an example on the next page.

about	for	on
against	in	with
at	of	

1. arrive _____ *at* _____

   arrive _____ *in* _____

   arrive _____ *on* _____

2. depend _____ *on* _____

3. remind _____ *About* _____

   remind

   remind _____ *For* _____

4. grow up _____ *in* _____

   grow up _____ *with* _____

5. compete _____ *for* _____

   compete _____ *Against* _____

   compete _____ *About* _____

   compete _____ *with* _____

DISCUSSION ACTIVITIES

Choose one or more of the following questions to discuss with your group members. Review the rules for group work your class created in the activity on page 10.

1. Make a link between Reading 1 and Reading 2. How are they related? With your group, make a list of the links between the two readings. Share your list with your classmates.

2. According to Reading 2, what are the advantages and disadvantages of "newcomer schools"? What other advantages and disadvantages can you think of that are not in the reading selection? With your group, make a list of the advantages and disadvantages. Share your list with your classmates.

3. Suppose your group is in charge of creating a program that will make the immigration experience easier for Generation 1.5 students. Include the following in your program:
   a. A title for the program
   b. Whom the program will serve
   c. What services will be included in the program
   d. How these services will help Generation 1.5 students

Share your ideas for your program with your classmates.

READING-RESPONSE JOURNAL

Choose one of the following topics, and write about it in your reading journal.

1. Have you ever felt "in between" like the Generation 1.5 immigrants? What are the advantages and disadvantages of being between two different groups?

2. What do you find "linkable" in this reading selection? Something may link up with your previous reading in this class or in others. Perhaps it links up with personal experience, something else you have read, or an idea you have heard of. Explain the linkages you see.

WRITING TOPICS

Choose one of the following topics, and write an essay.

1. What is one of the problems or challenges that Generation 1.5 students face? Give a specific example of this problem or challenge. Explain what you would do to solve the problem.

2. Do you know someone who is a Generation 1.5 immigrant? Are you a Generation 1.5 immigrant? Describe two ways in which the experiences of a real-life Generation 1.5 immigrant are similar to or different from what you have read.

3. Have you ever acted as a language broker? Describe your experience. Do you think it is a good idea for children to act as language brokers for their parents? Why or why not? If you have never acted as a language broker, what do you think the challenges and advantages might be?

Personal Impressions

READING 3

Prereading

Before you read, discuss the following questions with your classmates.

1. Some people immigrate to the United States for economic reasons. What are some other reasons people immigrate?

2. Leonid Yelin is from the former Soviet Union. What do you know about the former Soviet Union? What was the government like?

3. What do you know about the sport of volleyball? Have you ever played or watched a volleyball game?

Predicting

Before you read, do the following activities. They will help you predict what the reading selection will be about.

1. Read the first paragraph.

2. What do you think this reading selection will be about?

Previewing Specialized Vocabulary

Listed here are some of the specialized words that you will find in this reading selection. Knowing and understanding these words will help you understand the reading selection better.

- Review the definitions of these words.
- Identify which of these words, if any, you already know.
- Try to paraphrase the meaning of each word.
- Underline these words in the reading selection.

Soviet Union (*prop. n.*)—the Union of Soviet Socialist Republics, or USSR, a country in eastern Europe and northern Asia established in 1922 and dissolved in 1991, with Moscow as its capital (paragraph 1)

Tashkent (*prop. n.*)—capital city of Uzbekistan (paragraph 1)

Uzbekistan (*prop. n.*)—one of the republics that was formerly a part of the Soviet Union (paragraph 1)

volleyball (*n.*)—a sport played on a rectangular court by two teams that try to hit an inflated ball over a high net without letting it touch the ground (paragraph 1)

boot camp (*n. ph.*)—site of intensive physical training in preparation for military service (paragraph 2)

certificate stores (*n.*)—special stores in the former Soviet Union where only important government officials could shop (paragraph 3)

rampant (*adj.*)—widespread (paragraph 4)

poverty (*n.*)—the state of being poor (paragraph 4)

Apendix

capitalist barons (*n. ph.*)—businessmen who become rich by exploiting poor people (paragraph 4)

socialism (*n.*)—an economic system where all or nearly all resources and products are owned by a group of people or a centralized government (paragraph 6)

alien (*adj.*)—unknown or completely foreign (paragraph 13)

concept (*n.*)—idea (paragraph 13)

camaraderie (*n.*)—friendship and support (paragraph 14)

Leonid Yelin: An Immigrant's Story

1   Leonid Yelin was born in the Soviet Union in 1950, just as the Cold War was intensifying. He grew up in Tashkent, Uzbekistan (at that time, Uzbekistan was one of the fifteen Soviet republics). A promising athlete, Yelin received all the benefits of Soviet athletic training—perhaps the best athletic training in the world. Early on, he excelled[17] at several sports before dedicating[18] himself exclusively to volleyball at age seventeen.

2   His skill at the sport earned him opportunities not easily come by in Soviet society. At eighteen, when he, like all Soviet males, had to enter military service, Yelin was able to get into officers' school and avoid the harsher[19] boot camp simply because he was a good volleyball player. These schools sponsored sports teams. The best young players were allowed to fulfill their military obligations[20] by playing on military teams.

3   Later, as a star athlete, Yelin received other privileges not available to the common Soviet citizen. He was immediately provided with an apartment, instead of being placed on a years-long waiting list. He had a car, a luxury item in the USSR. And he had shopping privileges at one of the so-called certificate stores, closed to ordinary citizens, where he could buy scarce commodities such as choice meats, fresh fruits and vegetables in winter, American cigarettes, and imported electronics.

4   Yelin had grown up accepting what he read about the West in his schoolbooks and in *Pravda*, the state newspaper—the excessive crime, the rampant poverty, the greed of the capitalist barons destroying society and the environment, the cruel and unusual punishment inflicted on political prisoners. It was therefore "a big shock" to Yelin when his teammates would come back from tournaments in Europe saying that they had seen a West vastly different from the one depicted in Soviet publications and on Soviet television. He didn't immediately conclude that the government was lying, but he certainly found it hard to doubt the word of the people closest to him.

5   When his playing career was over, Yelin became a coach. As the head coach of Uzbekistan's women's volleyball team, he directed his team to the USSR Women's

---

[17]**to excel** (*v.*) — to do better than, to exceed
[18]**to dedicate** (*v.*) — to commit oneself to an idea or action
[19]**harsh** (*adj.*) — severe; unpleasant
[20]**obligations** (*n.*) — required responsibilities

Championship in 1978. Despite his success in sports, Yelin was not happy. His life was strictly controlled in many ways. He decided to apply for a visa to leave the Soviet Union. He wanted to go to America. He would have to give up a lot to leave the USSR. He knew that in the United States, volleyball didn't have the prestige[21] of other sports. He would have no status at all. But he wasn't seeking status or material wealth. He wanted more freedom for himself and his family. Yelin was willing to drive a taxi in America, he said. After months of completing the proper paperwork, he submitted his application to emigrate.

6   That is when his troubles began. He was dismissed from his position as coach. Next, the secret police called Yelin in for an "interview." The officials conducting the interview accused him of betraying[22] socialism. They showed him sworn statements, written by fellow teammates and coaches, denouncing[23] him as an enemy of socialism. After that, both Yelin and his wife were deprived[24] of their privileges and status. They were forced to take jobs well beneath their talents.

7   More than ever, Yelin wanted to leave the Soviet Union. With his daughter now seven years old and another child on the way, Yelin was thinking of his children's future. Despite the difficulties and the dangers, he applied once again to emigrate.

8   The whole procedure took months. He had to file many forms and documents. Bribes were necessary every step of the way. Finally, the day came when everything was in order. He went down to the emigration bureau to receive his visa.

9   Early in 1989, Leonid Yelin and his family left the Soviet Union. They received permission to enter the United States and flew to Miami, knowing nothing about the city except that it was warm and in America.

10   From the beginning of his new life, Yelin was willing to do whatever it took to support his family. He knew the work would be hard. He couldn't even speak a complete sentence in English. Within days of his arrival, he got his first job, laying tile in a new building. He knew nothing about tiling, but that didn't matter. It was money to support his family. But this part-time job paid very little money, much less than the minimum wage. He knew that this was a typical entry-level job for newly arrived immigrants. He also knew that he was being exploited, but for the time being, that didn't matter to Yelin. He was just happy to work.

11   Next came a better job: delivering pizzas. Yelin thought it was a good job because he was forced to speak English and to learn his way around the city. But he did not make enough money to cover expenses. Then one day he caught a break. A Russian friend who was working at a department store arranged for Yelin to interview for a sales job. The interview with the store's personnel manager lasted thirty long minutes, and Yelin understood almost nothing. He just kept nodding his head and saying, "Yes, ma'am." When he left the office, Yelin had no idea what had happened, so his friend went in to ask the personnel manager. When he came back out, he said, "Congratulations, Leonid, you got the job!"

12   But Yelin's surprise gave way to panic when he was taken to his assignment: the women's perfume counter. He stared in disbelief. He didn't know enough about

[21]**prestige** (*n.*) — high standing; honor; esteem
[22]**to betray** (*v.*) — to be disloyal
[23]**to denounce** (*v.*) — to speak ill of someone; to criticize
[24]**to deprive** (*v.*) — to take something away

perfume to sell it. To tell the truth, he didn't even know enough English to sell *any-thing*. His first impulse was to leave as fast as he could. But the assistant manager, a Cuban and an immigrant herself, understood Yelin's nervousness. "But Leonid," she encouraged him, "don't you have a family? You have to stay for them. At least get the first check."

13   So Yelin stayed, even though he was still scared to death. It was all so strange to him. The number and variety of products was overwhelming[25]. He had come from a place where stores sold only one brand—the government's brand—of a product. Usually, it was not even available. Now he was confronted with a glittering array of bottles, names, shiny boxes, scents, and colors. And he had to keep them all straight in his head, ready to answer a customer's questions politely. That was another thing he had to learn—how to sell something, how to wait on a customer. It was a completely alien concept to a person raised in the Soviet Union. He had to learn that in American stores, "the customer is always right." He had to practice "service with a smile."

14   It was hard work, but not as difficult as Yelin had imagined. For one thing, he soon discovered that in Miami's immigrant community, camaraderie prevailed[26], a spirit of helping one another out to pursue the American dream. Even though they worked on commission at the perfume counter, the salespeople did not compete with one another. They looked out for one another. On breaks, a retired school-teacher helped Leonid study English. The Cuban employees, themselves newcomers to capitalism, taught him the technical complexities of the cash register and credit card transactions. They helped him make sales, shared commissions with him, and covered for his mistakes. "I never met a bad person in Miami," he says.

15   For Leonid Yelin, the department store was like a school in American culture. While at work, he looked around the store at all the products and the busy shoppers, and he felt proud that he had come so far. Sometimes he missed coaching volleyball, but when he reflected on his newfound freedom and the wide-open future his children now had, the sacrifice seemed worth it. If he lived out his days as a salesclerk, he could be happy.

16   One day, a customer asked Yelin where he was from. The man asked more questions. He seemed especially interested in Yelin's coaching background. He wrote down the telephone number of a volleyball coach. Yelin called and talked to her. She asked him if he wanted to coach volleyball again. "Are you serious?" he asked. He was surprised.

17   That began Yelin's career as a coach in America. First, he coached a team of high school girls. They were very successful, and a university in Miami offered him the chance to coach a women's team at the collegiate level. In just three years, Yelin guided the team to the national championship. He was named national coach of the year. But his biggest victory, he says, came just a few days after the tournament, when he was sworn in as a U.S. citizen.

18   "I have been a national champion before," he told newspaper reporters. "Many times, in the Soviet Union. But this time is different, you know, because now I am national champion in my new nation."

---

[25]**overwhelming** (*adj.*) — powerful, almost too strong to bear
[26]**to prevail** (*v.*) — to win

READING SKILLS

EXERCISE 14   **Finding the Main Idea**

Answer the following questions, which focus on the main idea of the reading selection.

1. What can we learn from the story of Leonid Yelin's immigration?

2. Yelin had a very successful life in the Soviet Union. Why did he choose to emigrate?

3. What kinds of hardships did Yelin face when he came to the United States?

4. What point is the author is trying to make by using Leonid Yelin's life as an example?

EXERCISE 15   **Ordering Details**

The following are events that happened in Leonid Yelin's life. Number the events in the order in which they happened. Event number one has been done for you as an example.

_____   Leonid was interviewed by the secret police.

_____   Leonid took a job tiling.

_____   Leonid decided to leave the USSR.

_____   What Leonid's teammates told him about Western countries was different from what he had learned in school.

_____   Leonid became the coach of the women's national team in Uzbekistan.

_____   Leonid became a women's volleyball coach in the United States.

_____   Leonid had privileges in the Soviet Union because he was a good athlete.

_1_   Leonid excelled at several sports.

_10_   Leonid got a job selling perfume in a department store.

_____   Leonid and his family went to Miami.

_____   Leonid worked delivering pizza.

VOCABULARY SKILLS

EXERCISE 16   **Academic Word List**

The following words are frequently found in academic writing. Knowing these words will help you read all kinds of academic texts. The first list is of Academic Words that you have seen earlier in this book. You can find these words again in this reading selection. Make sure these words are in your vocabulary notebook. (See page 7 for information about how to make a vocabulary notebook.) Add any new information that you learn about these words to your vocabulary notebook. The number in parentheses indicates the paragraph in this reading selection where the word appears.

1. exclusively (1)
2. available (3, 13)
3. environment (4)
4. publications (4)
5. conclude (4)
6. emigrate (5), emigration (8), immigrants (10)
7. status (5)
8. assistant (12)
9. community (14)

The second list is of Academic Words that are new in this reading selection. Add these words to your vocabulary notebook. The number in parentheses indicates the paragraph in this reading selection where the word appears.

1. intensifying (1)
2. benefits (1)
3. teams (2)
4. item (3)
5. commodities (3)
6. seeking (5)
7. submitted (5)
8. conducting (6)
9. finally (8)
10. procedure (8)
11. file (8)
12. documents (8)
13. minimum (10)
14. exploited (10)
15. assignment (12)
16. concept (13)
17. commission (14)
18. credit (14)

EXERCISE 17 **Learning Academic Words**

Use your knowledge about the Academic Words to decide if each of the following statements is true or false. Write *T* for true and *F* for false.

F 1. If you have the *minimum* amount of time to do your work, you should wait to do it later.

F 2. If I have one *item*, I have many things.

T 3. If you want to lose weight, you might receive *benefits* from a low-calorie diet.

T 4. If you work on *commission*, you receive extra money if you sell more things.

T 5. Soccer, basketball, and baseball are all examples of *team* sports.

F 6. It is impossible to buy or sell a *commodity*.

T 7. If I *submitted* my homework, the teacher should have received it.

T 8. If you *conduct* an interview, the other person will be answering questions you ask.

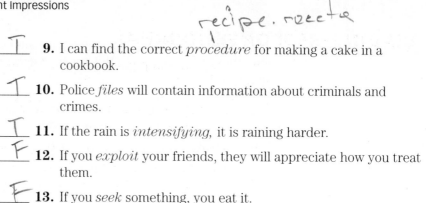

recipe · receta

__I__ **9.** I can find the correct *procedure* for making a cake in a cookbook.

__I__ **10.** Police *files* will contain information about criminals and crimes.

__I__ **11.** If the rain is *intensifying,* it is raining harder.

__F__ **12.** If you *exploit* your friends, they will appreciate how you treat them.

__F__ **13.** If you *seek* something, you eat it.

EXERCISE 18

Understanding Confusing Words

You have seen most of the following words in the reading selections in this chapter. These pairs of words are often confused. Study the meaning of each word. Write an original sentence that shows you know the meaning of each word.

immigrate *(v.)* — to move into a new country
emigrate *(v.)* — to move out of a country

effect *(n.)* — the result of a change
affect *(v.)* — to change

among *(prep.)* — linking three or more people or things
between *(prep.)* — linking two people or things

economic *(adj.)* — having to do with resources like money, labor, raw materials, and factories
economical *(adj.)* — providing good value for money, inexpensive

DISCUSSION ACTIVITIES

Choose one or more of the following questions to discuss with your group members. Review the rules for group work your class created in the activity on page 10.

1. Reread the description of the new immigrants on page 65. How is Leonid Yelin's immigration experience typical or not typical of the new immigrants described there?

2. What do you think would have happened to Leonid if he had not been able to immigrate to the United States?

3. Do an Internet search on Leonid Yelin. What is he doing now? Do you think he has been a successful immigrant? Explain your answer.

JRNAL

he following topics, and write about it in your reading

anyone who has been an immigrant like Leonid Yelin?
their immigrant experiences were similar or different.

mportant events that happened in Leonid Yelin's life.
do you think was the biggest change for him? Why do
is event was the biggest change?

he following topics, and write a composition.

went from being a star coach and national champion
t Union to tiling floors in the United States. Do you
ould have given up the prestige and the privileged,
life he formerly led in exchange for personal freedom?
r answer.

t you were Leonid Yelin's daughter or son. How would
t about his decision to come to the United States? Think
ration 1.5 children. Do you think it is difficult for them to
why their parents insist that they move to a new

internet activities, go to **elt.thomson.com/impressions**

Geography and Culture in the United States

Geography has helped shape American culture. The varied landscapes of North America have played an important role in the history of the nation. Land ownership and land use have been ongoing issues throughout this history. People in the United States are proud of the land they call "America the beautiful," a phrase that comes from the title of a favorite patriotic song. Most Americans also recognize the famous song quoted on this page, "This Land Is Your Land." They learn the song in school and enjoy singing it. Woody Guthrie's lyrics celebrate the rich diversity of the nation's geography. The lyrics also assert the fundamental principles of equal opportunity and democratic access to the land and its riches. But is this the whole story? Are those fundamental principles always acknowledged in reality?

> "This land is your land, this land is my land, From California to the New York Island, From the redwood forest to the Gulf Stream waters, This land was made for you and me."
>
> —Woody Guthrie, American folksinger

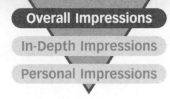
Overall Impressions

READING 1

Prereading

Before you read, discuss the following questions with your classmates.

1. What is the longest journey you have taken by automobile?

2. What does the expression "car-oriented culture" suggest to you?

3. What have you learned about regional differences in the United States?

Predicting

Before you read, do the following activities. They will help you predict what the reading selection will be about.

1. Look at the map on pages 96–97. Have you ever visited any of the places on the map? If not, have you heard of any of the places? What do you know about them?

2. The picture on page 95 shows examples of something called a "roadside attraction." Based on what you observe in the picture, what do you think is the purpose of such attractions?

Previewing Specialized Vocabulary

Listed here are some of the specialized words that you will find in this reading selection. Knowing and understanding these words will help you understand the reading selection better.

- Review the definitions of these words.
- Identify which of these words, if any, you already know.
- Try to paraphrase the meaning of each word.
- Underline these words in the reading selection.

legendary (*adj.*)—well-known, famous (paragraph 1)

sightseeing (*n.*)—visiting places of interest (paragraph 1)

vast (*adj.*)—large in area, immense (paragraph 1)

Indian (*n.*)—term used for referring to native peoples in North America (paragraph 2)

gimmicks (*n.*)—eye-catching tricks used to promote a business (paragraph 2)

forerunner (*n.*)—someone or something that appears first, a predecessor (paragraph 2)

interstate freeways (*n. ph.*)—a system of wide, high-speed highways that cross the United States (paragraph 3)

Dwight Eisenhower (*prop. n.*)—president of the United States from 1953 to 1961 (paragraph 3)

homogeneous (*adj.*)—similar, all the same (paragraph 6)

Homework. Nex class.

Road Trip, USA

1   One popular American activity is the road trip. A road trip is a sightseeing vacation taken by car. Such vacations are made possible by the nation's vast system of interstate highways. Some of the original cross-country highways have legendary status in American popular culture. Historically, the most renowned[1] highway was Route 66, a 2,450-mile-long road stretching from Chicago to Los Angeles (that's almost 4,000 kilometers). To this day, Route 66 is called the "Mother Road" because of its importance. It is celebrated in songs, in books, on television shows, and in movies. There are even clubs devoted to memorializing[2] the Mother Road.

2   After World War II, Route 66 became a popular tourist highway for Americans. As they drove the long highway, travelers enjoyed stopping to visit "roadside attractions." A roadside attraction, sometimes also called a "tourist trap," is designed to lure travelers into stopping and spending money. Part of Route 66's fame is associated with its unusual attractions. For example, along the highway there were motels shapes like teepees[3], American Indian souvenir shops, reptile farms, and amusingly designed hamburger stands. Gimmicks such as these were the forerunner of today's larger-scale attractions. For example, many of today's theme parks were inspired by the success of these roadside attractions. Mile after mile, Route 66 gave travelers a peek at unusual aspects of American culture.

Señuelo

3   Today, Route 66 no longer exists as an official highway. It has been replaced by interstate freeways. Beginning in the 1950s, the United States started building

[1]**renowned** (*adj.*) — famous
[2]**to memorialize** (*v.*) — to preserve the memory of something
[3]**teepees** (*n.*) — American Indian-style dwellings, originally made of buffalo hide stretched on a frame of wooden poles so as to form an inverted cone

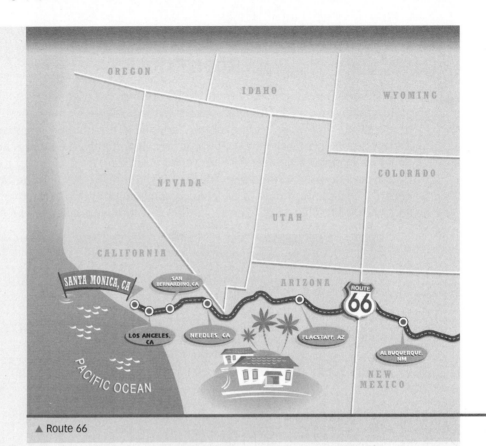

▲ Route 66

wide, efficient freeways. They were new highways without any stop signs or stop-lights. The president at the time, Dwight Eisenhower, had been a general in the Army during World War II. He wanted a good network of roads that the military could use for the rapid transport. Today, the interstate freeways are used mainly by commercial trucks and private cars.

Car Culture

4   During the summer months, Americans like to "load up the car" and "head out on the open road." Car commercials show how important mobility is to Americans. Many commercials show families or individuals driving to places far from civiliza-tion. They show Americans enjoying the sense of freedom that their car suppos-edly offers. This spirit of adventure is also quite evident in American films. Movies frequently use the road trip as a plot device. *Easy Rider* (1968), *Rain Man* (1989), *Thelma and Louise* (1991), and *Little Miss Sunshine* (2006) are popular examples of such films. Judging from the values displayed in television commercials and movies, the United States is a car-oriented culture.

Mobility and Diversity

5   Sociologists have asked an interesting question about America's car culture: Has a high degree of mobility affected regional diversity in the United States? Histor-ically, Americans have celebrated their social and cultural differences. Different regions are proud of the qualities that make them unique. In traveling around the

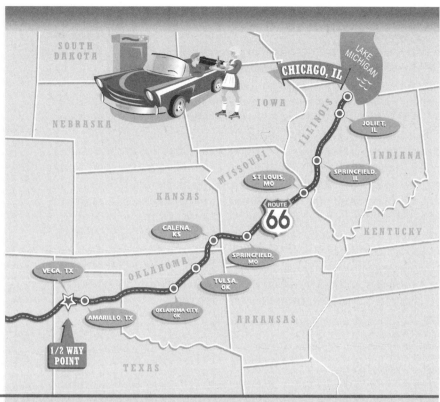

▲ Route 66 (*continued*)

country, Americans have learned that New England, the South, the Midwest, and the Far West are distinct. Over time, however, Americans have moved from one place to another. The regional differences are not as great as they used to be. Today, Massachusetts and Mississippi do not seem as different from each other as they once did.

6   Different regions have become more homogeneous. This is especially true along interstate freeways. Today, on a road trip across the United States, travelers might notice how similar different parts of the country have become. The same restaurants, gas stations, and hotels are found along the freeways. Another example of similarity is in the architecture. For instance, shopping centers around the country look basically the same. The different regions are becoming similar in other ways, too. A handful of companies dominate radio and television. This means that Americans hear and watch nearly identical programming everywhere in the United States. There is even a national newspaper, *USA Today*, available everywhere.

7   Despite this superficial uniformity, however, an observant[4] visitor to the United States might still notice regional differences. Even though these differences are not as pronounced as they once were, they are still there. Some differences concern behavior and attitudes. For instance, in the Northeast, life is often fast-paced[5]. People tend to be in a hurry. Sometimes they seem curt[6]. In the South, on

[4]**observant** (*adj.*) — paying close attention
[5]**fast paced** (*adj.*) — energetic, active, busy
[6]**curt** (*adj.*) — brief in speech to the point of seeming rude

the other hand, life is slower-paced[7], and greater emphasis is placed on courtesy[8]. The West Coast is famously "laid back" in comparison to other regions. In contrast, the people of the Midwest are considered industrious[9], straightforward[10], and conservative. These are generalizations, of course, that don't apply to everybody.

8   Climate varies from region to region as well. The West is generally dry. The Midwest experiences the greatest extremes in temperature. It has hot summers and cold winters. The Northeast is cool or cold much of the year, with a relatively short growing season. The South is temperate in the winter and hot in the summer. This allows for the cultivation of crops such as tobacco, rice, and cotton in the South. Historically, the South developed a more agricultural economy than the industrial northern states. This fundamental difference in economy led to stark differences between North and South on the issue of slavery. In the middle of the nineteenth century, the northern states and the southern states fought a civil war over the issue that lasted four years (1861–1865).

9   One of the world's largest countries, the United States is geographically and culturally diverse. Americans will tell you that there's no better way to experience this diversity than by taking a road trip from coast to coast.

---

[7]**slower-paced** (*adj.*) — relaxed, unhurried
[8]**courtesy** (*n.*) — good manners, proper etiquette
[9]**industrious** (*adj.*) — hardworking
[10]**straightforward** (*adj.*) — honest, direct

READING SKILLS

EXERCISE 1   **Finding the Main Idea**

Match the main idea with each paragraph. The first one has been done for you as an example.

_6_   Different regions of the United States have become more homogeneous.

_2_   Part of Route 66's fame came from the roadside attractions.

_3_   Interstate freeways have replaced highways like Route 66.

_8_   Climate affects the different regions in the United States.

_1_   Historically, Route 66 is one of the most famous American highways.

_7_   There are still differences among the people in different regions in the United States.

_4_   America's car culture is reflected in commercials and popular films.

_5_   The car culture has lessened regional differences.

EXERCISE 2   **Reading for Details**

Answer the following questions using details from the reading selection.

1. Why is Route 66 called the Mother Road?

2. What are some roadside attractions that were found on Route 66?

3. Why did President Eisenhower replace highways with interstate freeways?

4. What do Americans do that shows that they live in a car-oriented culture?

5. In what ways have the different regions of the United States become homogeneous?

6. What kinds of differences in behavior and attitudes exist in various regions of the United States?

7. Explain how the different regions of the United States differ in climate.

EXERCISE 3   **Reading Maps**

Look at the map on pages 96–97, and answer the following questions.

1. What were the starting and ending cities on Route 66?

2. What states did Route 66 go through?

3. What was the halfway point on Route 66?

4. Which state had the shortest portion of Route 66 going through it?

5. How many states did Route 66 go through?

VOCABULARY SKILLS

EXERCISE 4   **Academic Word List**

The following words are frequently found in academic writing. Knowing these words will help you read all kinds of academic texts. The first list is of Academic Words that you have seen earlier in this book. You can find these words again in this reading selection. Make sure these words are in your vocabulary notebook. (See page 7 for information about how to make a vocabulary notebook.) Add any new information that you learn about these words to your vocabulary notebook. The number in parentheses indicates the paragraph in this reading selection where the word appears.

1. status (1)	3. devoted (1)	6. military (3)
2. culture (1), cultural (5), culturally (10)	4. designed (2)	7. individuals (4)
	5. aspects (2)	8. displayed (4) ~ *Exposition*

9. device (4)

10. affected (5)

11. regional (5), regions (5)

12. diversity (5), diverse (9) – Vamos, diversos

13. unique (5)

14. distinct (5)

15. similar (6), similarities (6)

16. available (6)

17. uniformity (7)

18. attitudes (7)

19. emphasis (7)

20. varies (8)

21. economy (8)

The second list is of Academic Words that are new in this reading selection. Add these words to your vocabulary notebook. The number in parentheses indicates the paragraph in this reading selection where the word appears.

1. route (1)

2. network (3)

3. transport (3)

4. evident (4)

5. oriented (4)

6. dominate (6)

7. identical (6)

8. despite (7)

9. instance (7)

10. straightforward (7)

11. fundamental (8)

12. issue (8)

13. civil (8)

EXERCISE 5

Learning Academic Words

Some words have several meanings. Look at the dictionary entries for the following Academic Words. Choose the meaning that best fits how the word is used in this reading selection.

1. route
   a. A road, course, or way for travel from one place to another
   b. A highway
   c. A customary way of travel
   d. A fixed territory assigned to a salesperson or delivery person

2. network
   a. A system of lines or channels that cross or interconnect
   b. An extended group of people with similar interests or concerns who interact and remain in informal contact for mutual assistance or support
   c. A chain of radio or television broadcasting stations linked by wire or microwave relay
   d. A system of computers interconnected by telephone wires or other means in order to share information

3. civil
   a. Relating to a citizen or citizens
   b. Relating to citizens and their relationships with the government
   c. Polite
   d. Relating to laws of society that are not criminal laws

4. device
  a. A machine
  b. A technique
  c. A plan
  d. A decorative design

ZOTH
LOVE.
62 and 64

5. issue
  a. Something published or produced
  b. A matter of discussion or debate
  c. A personal problem
  d. A single copy of a magazine

EXERCISE 6

Practicing with Adjectives

Adjectives are words that describe people, places, or things.

- Look at the following list of adjectives.
- Which adjectives end with *ing*? Which end with *ed*? Which end with *al*?
- Are all words that end with *ing*, *ed*, or *al* adjectives?
- Find the following adjectives in the reading selection. After each word, write the word it describes and the meaning of the phrase.

The first one has been done for you as an example.

1. sightseeing *vacation—a vacation taken for pleasure to see*
    different attractions

2. original — unique.

3. renowned — Famous.

4. unusual — unique - different.

5. amusing — Interesting.

6. commercial — Propaganda.

7. car-oriented — utes a lot

8. regional — Region - state . Centain Area

9. superficial — Fake —

10. fast-paced — Everything done quickly
    life Quickly.

11. slower-paced — slower pace) — slow life
12. agricultural — Agricola
13. industrial —
14. fundamental — basic

DISCUSSION ACTIVITIES

Form a group of three or four students. Review the rules for group work your class created in the activity on page 10. Do one of the following activities.

1. Compared to some other countries, the United States does not have a good public transportation system. In some U.S. cities, a car is a necessity. With your group members, list the disadvantages of a car-oriented culture. Explain why you believe they are disadvantages. Compare your group's list with others in your class.

2. In your opinion, which is more valuable to a society: uniformity—for example, everyone speaking the same language—or diversity? With your classmates, list reasons why each is more valuable.

3. Think about how different regions of the United States are presented in Hollywood movies (the South, the Northeast, the West, the Midwest). Your teacher can help you think of movies about different regions. What have you learned about these regions from watching movies? Do you think the movies are accurate in their presentation?

READING-RESPONSE JOURNAL

Choose one of the following topics, and write about it in your journal.

1. What do you find practical or useful in this reading selection? How can the reading selection help you understand how Americans feel about their cars?

2. Can you link the ideas in this reading selection to your own experiences? Are regional differences disappearing in your native country? Why, in your opinion, is this process happening?

STUDENT IMPRESSIONS

The following paragraphs were written by students attending colleges in the United States. Each student comments on transportation issues he or she has learned about while studying in the United States.

Students Reflect on America's Car Culture

Dar, proporcionar

Gabriella Augusztin: "Sitting outside at New York's John F. Kennedy Airport, I was exhausted from the twelve-hour flight, and the last couple of hours that seemed endless while I waited for the bus to pick me up. It was four o'clock in the morning back in Hungary. I was extremely tired and cold from the air conditioning. 'Is this what it's like in the country of opportunities and freedom?' I thought. Then another thought crossed my mind: These cars are sure big! Very quickly, I realized that not only the cars are huge in this country but also the amount of food, the size of furniture, and the distances are huge as well. The streets were wider than anywhere I have ever been. The buildings were taller. But the weirdest thing was on the streets—or actually, what wasn't on the streets: people. There were no pedestrians. Instead of feeling like I was in wonderland, I felt like I was in outer space."

Choi-Yee Kwong: "Transportation is very inconvenient in San Francisco because sometimes people have to wait for the bus for an hour. So many people have a car since it is cheap to buy a car. On the other hand, in Hong Kong, a car is very expensive, and most people can't afford to buy a car. However, the public transportation is very convenient in Hong Kong. People only need to wait five or ten minutes for the bus."

Haw Hsiang Hsu: "Transportation and parking in Taiwan is more convenient than in California. Taiwan is a small land, so when we try to get somewhere, it is easy for us to take public transportation, such as a bus, a taxi, or MRT (mass rapid transportation). For private transportation, we ride motorcycles or bicycles most of the time, so it is easy to park or go somewhere. But here in California, you have to drive your own car everywhere. Right now, it is very hard for me to drive. Because I am a new driver, I think it is too dangerous for me."

Giuseppe Novelli: "One of the biggest failings of the United States is cars. It's something I will never understand. Everybody goes by car, *everywhere*. You can find these enormous SUVs rumbling in these huge roads. Honestly, they make the landscape really look terrible. Also, we need to take a minute to reflect on oil and the consequential relationship with the Middle East. Cars cause too many problems."

WRITING TOPICS

Choose one of the following topics, and write about it.

1. What are the advantages and disadvantages of American car culture? Give specific examples to support your opinion. See "Student Impressions" for examples.

2. Describe a road trip or a journey that you have taken. Explain why this journey was significant to you.

3. Write an essay that identifies and explains the advantages of a good public transportation system.

4. Do movies and advertisements reflect the values of the culture in which they are produced? Give some examples to support your response.

In-Depth Impressions

READING 2

Prereading

Before you read, discuss the following questions with your classmates.

1. What does the word *myth* mean? How do we commonly use the word?

2. What comes to mind when you think of the "American West"?

3. Where have these ideas come from? Schoolbooks? Television? Movies?

Predicting

Before you read, do the following activities. They will help you predict what the reading selection will be about.

1. The following reading selection comes from a history textbook. Knowing this, what do you expect from the reading?

2. What does the word *frontier* mean? How is the American West associated with the frontier?

Previewing Specialized Vocabulary

Listed here are some of the specialized words that you will find in this reading selection. Knowing and understanding these words will help you understand the reading selection better.

- Review the definitions of these words.
- Identify which of these words, if any, you already know.
- Try to paraphrase the meaning of each word.
- Underline these words in the reading selection.

stereotyped (*v.*)—characterized by an overly simple conception (paragraph 1)

cowboys (*n.*)—hired men who care for cattle (cows, bulls, and calves) (paragraph 1)

pioneers (*n.*)—people who enter into new lands to settle them (paragraph 1)

idealized (*adj.*)—regarded or perceived in ideal form (paragraph 2)

ranchers (*n.*)—owners or managers of ranches (paragraph 2)

legend (*n.*)—a story that is popularly believed to be historically accurate (paragraph 2)

Buffalo Bill Cody (*prop. n.*)—a famous showman in the nineteenth century (paragraph 3)

frontiersman (*n.*)—a man who lives and works beyond the boundary of civilization (paragraph 4)

army scout (*n. ph.*)—a soldier who goes in advance of the main army to gather information (paragraph 4)

> **frontier** (*n.*)—an undeveloped area beyond the places where people have settled (paragraph 5)
> **overlooked** (*v.*)—failed to notice (paragraph 5)
> **herds** (*n.*)—large groups (paragraph 7)

Myths of the American West

1   Each of the distinct regions of the United States has become stereotyped in the popular imagination to some extent. No region, however, has been the source of so  many myths as the American West. Around the world, this region is associated with cowboys, Indians, pioneers, and deserts. While there is some truth to this popular image, the reality is much more complex.

2   An idealized view of the American West has been part of popular culture for more than a century. In the nineteenth century, this mythic West appeared in novels, songs, and paintings. In the twentieth century, movies, radio programs, television shows, and advertising continued the mythmaking. The legend of the American West has had far-reaching influence.

3   In the middle of the nineteenth century, "dime novels" helped popularize this legend. One dime novel, *Buffalo Bill: King of the Border Men* (1869), was especially important. It created an idealized hero out of the real-life figure of William F. ("Buffalo Bill") Cody. In the novel, Cody is presented as a powerful agent for morality and social order. In scene after scene, the novel shows him driving off dangerous Indians and rounding up horse thieves and no-good cattle rustlers[11].

4   The reading public loved this portrayal of a "typical" western frontiersman. In turn, the real-life Cody was inspired in 1883 to imitate the legendary accounts of his life. He started a traveling exhibition that he called the "Wild West Show." Cody was a former army scout and pony express rider[12]. He was also a natural showman, and his exhibitions proved immensely popular. Cody and his group presented mock[13] battles between army scouts and Indians. The Wild West Show taught Americans to think of the American West as a morality drama of good versus evil. It reinforced the popular image of the West as a "wild" arena[14] where good always triumphed in its encounter with evil.

5   In the decades that followed, stories, paintings, and movies repeated the myths started by the Wild West Show. This Western myth had many contributors. It was the collective work of dime-novel writers, newspaper reporters, railroad publicists[15], politicians, artists, and movie directors. The myth, however, was far removed

---

[11]**cattle rustlers** (*n.*) — people who steal cows
[12]**pony express rider** (*n.*) — in the nineteenth century, a person who delivered mail over long distances on horseback
[13]**mock** (adj.) — make-believe, not real
[14]**arena** (*n.*) — a stadium where a performance or a competition is held
[15]**publicists** (*n.*) — hired promoters

from the actual reality of the West. The idealized description of the West ignored the darker experiences of frontier expansion. This was especially true when it came to the native people. The myths didn't include the cruel treatment of Indians and the forced removal of the Indians to reservations. They also overlooked the racist discrimination against Mexican-Americans and blacks. The myths usually didn't include other realities of life in the West either. For example, the risks of commercial agriculture and cattle raising were not usually mentioned.

6   Even today, many Americans accept the legend of the West as a paradise. They believe it represents a simple, pure life. Many Americans still believe that this is what the West was like before cities, factories, and masses of immigrants.

7   The reality of westward expansion was more complex. Nineteenth-century Americans used the army to drive out the Indians. They exploited the region's vast natural resources without thinking of the consequences. In less than thirty years, they killed off the enormous buffalo herds. They depleted[16] the region's deposits of gold and silver. They also plowed up[17] the prairie grasslands into farms. Large mines, ranches, and huge farm businesses shoved aside the small miners and farmers and took control of much of the natural resources of the area. The mythic view of the frontier West has covered up this dark side of the expansion.

8   Despite this problem with reality, the settlement of the West had some benefits. The West reinforced the popular image of the United States as a place of economic opportunity and democracy. Although the poor treatment of blacks, Indians, and Spanish-speaking Americans contradicted the idea of an open society, eventually

▲ American Indians displaced from their homelands

[16]**to deplete** (*v.*) — to use up, to reduce the supply of something
[17]**to plow up** (*v.*) — to dig out of the ground

these things began to change. New towns began to grow. In these towns, people of different races lived together. People's attitudes about others began to change.

9   The mythic view of the West hid the more cruel and destructive features of western expansionism. However, the experiences gained from settling the West eventually led to the beginnings of the conservation movement. People began to reassess the traditional American views of the environment. They saw the value in the beauty of the wild land. The U.S. government set aside land, protecting the natural plants and animals. The West had other positive effects on the United States. By the beginning of the twentieth century, the thriving[18] farms, ranches, mines, and cities in the West helped make the United States into one of the world's most prosperous nations.

[18]**thriving** (*adj.*) — successful, productive

READING SKILLS

EXERCISE 7

Finding the Main Idea

The main idea of this reading selection is the last sentence of the first paragraph: "While there is some truth to this popular image, the reality is much more complex." The rest of the reading selection has details that support the main idea. Working with a partner, underline sentences in the text that support the main idea.

EXERCISE 8

Recognizing Fact or Opinion

Everything that we hear or read is composed of both facts and opinions. An important skill for every student is to recognize the difference between fact and opinion. Reading 2 is a good example of academic writing that uses both fact and opinion. The following statements are taken from the reading. Write *F* for the statements of fact and *O* for the statements of opinion.

__O__ **1.** The legend of the American West has had far-reaching influence.

__O__ **2.** Buffalo Bill Cody started a traveling exhibition that he called the "Wild West Show."

__F__ **3.** While seemingly providing entertainment, the Wild West Show reinforced the popular image of the West as a "wild" arena where good always triumphed in its encounter with evil.

__O__ **4.** The idealized description of the West ignored the darker experience of frontier expansion.

__O__ **5.** Even today, many Americans accept the legend of the West as a paradise.

__O__ **6.** Nineteenth-century Americans used the army to drive out the Indians.

_____ **7.** The West had other positive effects on the United States. By the beginning of the twentieth century, the thriving farms, ranches, mines, and cities in the West helped make the United States into one of the world's most prosperous nations.

VOCABULARY SKILLS

EXERCISE 9

Academic Word List

The following words are frequently found in academic writing. Knowing these words will help you read all kinds of academic texts. The first list is of Academic Words that you have seen earlier in this book. You can find these words again in this reading selection. Make sure these words are in your vocabulary notebook. (See page 7 for information about how to make a vocabulary notebook.) Add any new information that you learn about these words to your vocabulary notebook. The number in parentheses indicates the paragraph in this reading selection where the word appears.

1. created (3)

2. drama (4)

3. encounter (4)

4. contributors (5)

5. discrimination (5)

6. immigrants (6)

7. area (7)

8. enormous (7)

9. benefits (8)

10. economic (8)

11. contradicted (8)

12. features (9) *caracteriztica - Rasgo*

13. traditional (9)

14. environment (9)

The second list is of Academic Words that are new in this reading selection. Add these words to your vocabulary notebook. The number in parentheses indicates the paragraph in this reading selection where the word appears.

1. image (1)

2. complex (1)

3. parallel (2)

4. exhibitions (4)

5. reinforce (4)

6. decades (5)

7. removed (5), removal (5)

8. ignored (5)

9. expansion (5), expansionism (9)

10. exploited (7)

11. consequences (7)

12. reassess (9)

13. positive (9)

14. effects (9)

EXERCISE 10

Recognizing Opposites

Match each Academic Word with its opposite.

complex

parallel

created

reinforce

expansion

enormous

traditional

positive

1. _Expansion_ contraction

2. _Reinforce_ weaken

3. _Parallel_ dissimilar

4. _created_ destroyed

5. _Enormous_ tiny

6. _Positive_ negative

7. _traditional_ innovative

8. _Complex_ simple

EXERCISE 11 **Using Phrasal Verbs**

Discuss with your classmates the meaning of the word *look*. What do the words *look up* mean? *Look up* is an example of a phrasal verb. Phrasal verbs are verbs joined with a participle. Meaning is important in phrasal verbs because the two words together can have a very different meaning from the meaning of each individual word. Find the following phrasal verbs in the reading selection. Write a definition of each phrasal verb. Compare your definitions with those of your classmates.

1. driving off (paragraph 3)

_____

2. rounding up (paragraph 3)

_____

3. killed off (paragraph 7)

_____

4. plowed up (paragraph 7)

_____

5. covered up (paragraph 7)

_____

What other phrasal verbs do you know? With your classmates, make a list of all the phrasal verbs you can think of.

DISCUSSION ACTIVITIES

Form a group of three or four students. Review the rules for group work your class created in the activity on page 10. Do one of the following activities. Share the results of your group discussion with your classmates.

1. Make a list of popular ideas about cowboys. Where have those ideas come from?

2. This reading selection appears in a high school textbook used in the United States. We expect textbooks to provide facts. This selection mixes opinions with facts. Make a list of the author's opinions.

READING-RESPONSE JOURNAL

Choose one of the following topics, and write about it in your journal.

1. Are you familiar with another country besides the United States whose regions are the subject of myths and stereotypes? Explain.

2. Is it important for history textbooks to discuss the "dark side" of a nation's history? Do textbooks usually do this?

WRITING TOPICS

Choose one of the following topics, and write about it.

1. The mythic version of the American West has been popular around the world. In your opinion, why do people outside the United States enjoy western stories so much?

2. In the United States, people value an open society where opportunity is freely available to everyone. From what you have learned, do you think the history of the American West has upheld this value or not?

Personal Impressions

READING 3

Prereading

Before you read, discuss the following questions with your classmates.

1. Share with your classmates some of your memories of family vacations.

2. What do you remember about Route 66 from Reading 1 in this chapter?

Predicting

Before you read, do the following activities. They will help you predict what the reading selection will be about.

1. What is a memoir? Why do people write memoirs? What kind of story do you expect when you see the word *memoir* in the title?

2. What does the word *nostalgia* mean? People sometimes have a *selective memory* of the past. That is, they remember only the good things about the past while forgetting some of the bad things. Do you know anyone like this, someone who frequently speaks about the "good old days"?

Previewing Specialized Vocabulary

Listed here are some of the specialized words that you will find in this reading selection. Knowing and understanding these words will help you understand the reading selection better.

- Review the definitions of these words.
- Identify which of these words, if any, you already know.
- Try to paraphrase the meaning of each word.
- Underline these words in the reading selection.

siblings (*n.*)—brothers and sisters (paragraph 1)

monotonous (*adj.*)—always the same, boring (paragraph 2)

profound impact (*n. ph.*)—a strong impression (paragraph 3)

hamlet (*n.*)—a very small town (paragraph 3)

franchise (*n.*)—an individual business authorized to use the name and sell the products of a larger corporation (paragraph 3)

Indian trading posts (*n. ph.*)—stores located in an underpopulated area that trades supplies for local products (paragraph 3)

mesmerized (*adj.*)—entranced, completely fascinated (paragraph 4)

snow flurries (*n. ph.*)—light snowfall (paragraph 4)

diner (*n.*)—an inexpensive restaurant, usually serving travelers or workers (paragraph 4)

neon (*n.*)—a gas used to make brightly colored lights (paragraph 4)

hunkered down (*v. ph.*)—took shelter during a storm (paragraph 5)

wee hours (*n. ph.*)—the earliest hours of the morning, before dawn (paragraph 5)

Memoir of a Road Trip

1   During my grade school years, my family lived cross-country from my parents' native Southern California. Every year, though there was too little money and not enough time, an inevitable longing overcame my parents as the holidays approached. It was Christmas, and they wanted nothing more than to be in California with their parents and siblings. — hermanos/as.

2   In those days, the way west followed Route 66. Beginning in Chicago, the great highway unraveled in quirky curves and twists and long straight-aways all the way to California. There was nothing monotonous about it. Each mile revealed something unusual, something worthy of a postcard or a father's comment: "Hey, kids, will you look at that? Now there's something you don't see every day." It could be anything—a motor court[19] of concrete teepees, a roadside attraction featuring rattlesnakes, or the world's largest totem pole[20]. The endless wonders of Route 66 gave the highway a mythic stature no other American road can claim.

3   For me, a small boy, those long drives west had a profound impact. I recall sitting in the back seat wiping mist off the cold pane to stare at the landscape unfolding before me. Those were the days before interstate freeways turned travel into an enervating repetition of identical interchanges—the same fast-food franchises, the same hotel chains whether you are in Georgia or Minnesota. Back then, highway travel was charged with a kind of magic: each town held out the promise of something new, something different, and quite possibly something astonishing. For one thing, the old highways routed you right through every little town—right down Main Street, in fact, where the eccentricities[21] of each isolated hamlet were displayed to the traveler. And since you were forced to slow down from sixty to twenty-five miles per hour (maybe even forced to sit for thirty seconds at the town's only stoplight), you got a glimpse of things strange and wonderful. Who knew what would come next: an Indian trading post perhaps, or a ghost town[22] graveyard, or a couple of giant arrows stuck in the ground for no apparent reason.

4   I was mesmerized by the journey. In my memory, the ride out Route 66 remains a series of stirring sights. I remember snow flurries whipping the Christmas

[19]**motor court** (*n. ph.*) — motel, roadside hotel
[20]**totem pole** (*n.*) — a tall pole carved with decorative motifs
[21]**eccentricities** (*n.*) — unusual behaviors or aspects
[22]**ghost town** (*n. ph.*) — an abandoned town, no longer inhabited

decorations hung from lampposts in small Oklahoma towns. I remember the neon lights of Tucumcari's motel strip, electric saguaros[23] and bucking broncos[24] ticking on and off in the desert night. I remember the beautiful, mysterious sound of the word "Albuquerque" on signposts—then the city itself, with its chicken yards and adobe hovels[25], unlike anything I'd ever seen before. There were Indian trading posts set against the red rock cliffs of Gallup. And there was a chilly diner in Flagstaff on a day so bitter the food was cold before the waitress could serve it.

5   The critical point of the journey came somewhere in Arizona, the sun sinking low on our third or fourth day on the road. After whispered front-seat discussions, my parents would turn to us and ask if we wanted to stop at a motel or drive through the night to Los Angeles. By then, our excitement was uncontainable. Bouncing on the seat, we chorused for California. My father—having already put in a six hundred-mile day—hunkered down for the final two-fifty. Despite the fervor inspired by imminent arrival, I eventually fell asleep in the back seat, knowing that come what may, my father would get us to L.A. before dawn. Sometime in the middle of the night, I stirred momentarily when he cracked the window and warm desert air rushed in over my face. Then in the wee hours, I found myself being lifted from the car, a perfume of citrus and oleander[26] and eucalyptus[27] filling my nostrils with the scent of California, the scent, for me, of Christmas.

[23]**saguaros** (*n.*) — a type of cactus
[24]**bucking broncos** (*n. ph.*) — wild horses known for kicking with their rear legs
[25]**adobe hovels** (*n. ph.*) — small houses made from a plaster of dried mud
[26]**oleander** (*n.*) — a bush with red or white flowers
[27]**eucalyptus** (*n.*) — a tree with aromatic leaves

READING SKILLS

EXERCISE 12   ## Finding the Main Idea

Reading 3 is an example of narrative writing. Narrative writing is different from academic writing. Storytelling is more important than making a particular point or attempting to persuade the reader. Nevertheless, narrative writing often communicates a subtle or implicit point. A good reader can identify the sentences that suggest the theme or main point of the narrative. In the memoir that you have just read, find the five sentences that you think are most important in communicating the theme of the story. Compare your choices with those of a fellow student.

Sentence 1:

_____

_____

Sentence 2:

_____

_____

Sentence 3:

_____

_____

Sentence 4:

_____

_____

Sentence 5:

_____

_____

VOCABULARY SKILLS

EXERCISE 13 **Academic Word List**

The following words are frequently found in academic writing. Knowing these words will help you read all kinds of academic texts. The first list is of Academic Words that you have seen earlier in this book. You can find these words again in this reading selection. Make sure these words are in your vocabulary notebook. (See page 7 for information about how to make a vocabulary notebook.) Add any new information that you learn about these words to your vocabulary notebook. The number in parentheses indicates the paragraph in this reading selection where the word appears.

1. featuring (2) **2.** series (4) **3.** eventually (5)

The second list is of Academic Words that are new in this reading selection. Add these words to your vocabulary notebook. The number in parentheses indicates the paragraph in this reading selection where the word appears.

1. approached (1) **5.** impact (3) **8.** couple (3)

2. inevitable (1) **6.** routed (3) **9.** apparent (3)

3. revealed (2) **7.** isolated (3) **10.** final (5)

4. comment (2)

EXERCISE 14 **Reviewing the Different Forms of a Word**

The following charts contain lists of Academic Words from the reading selections in this chapter. When you learn new words, you should also try to learn the different forms the word can take, depending on its function in a sentence. This activity will help improve your comprehension and expand your vocabulary. Fill in the correct forms for each blank.

Verbs	Past, Perfect, and Passive Form	Present, Third-Person Singular	Gerund Form as a Noun	Noun Form
Base Word	**Add -ed**	**Add -s or -es**	**Add -ing**	
approach	approached	approaches	approaching	approach
reveal — Revelar.				
reassess				
remove				
exploit				
devote				
orient				
dominate				
display				
transport				

Nouns	Plural	Adjective
Base Word	**Ends in -s, -es, -ies**	**Ends in -al, -ic, -ical, -ory, etc.**
culture		
image		
drama		
region		
consequence		
benefit		
tradition		
economy		
contradiction		
environment		

EXERCISE 15 **Recognizing Related Words**

Each group of four words includes one word that does not belong. Cross out the unrelated word. Academic Words from the reading passages are in bold.

1. **evident**	obvious	hidden	clear
2. **create**	construct	destroy	build
3. **image**	picture	portrait	object
4. **route**	highway	field	path
5. **comment**	gesture	statement	speech
6. **reinforce**	support	drop	sustain
7. **isolated**	distant	nearby	remote
8. **complex**	difficult	simple	complicated
9. **straight-forward**	clear	direct	roundabout
10. **dominate**	allow	dictate	control

DISCUSSION ACTIVITIES

Form a group of three or four students. Review the rules for group work your class created in the activity on page 10. Discuss one of the following topics.

1. Why does the boy in the story enjoy the long trip across the country?

2. Have you ever taken a long trip? Describe your journey to your classmates.

READING-RESPONSE JOURNAL

Choose one of the following topics, and write about it in your journal.

1. Does this memoir remind you of a trip you have taken? Describe the trip.

2. Describe other memoirs that you have read. What event in your life would you write a memoir about? Why did you choose that event?

WRITING TOPICS

Choose one of the following topics, and write a composition.

1. Describe an occasion when you were homesick.

2. The writer associates certain smells with the holiday of Christmas. Do you associate smells with a holiday of importance to you?

INTERNET ACTIVITIES

For additional internet activities, go to **elt.thomson.com/impressions**

Musical Impressions

In Chapter 2, you read a poem by Walt Whitman called "I Hear America Singing." In the poem, Whitman spoke about the music created by common people as they go about their daily activities. This, Whitman felt, was the true source of American music. As the quotation on this page suggests, George Gershwin, a renowned American composer, agreed with Whitman. In the United States, creative and original music has often emerged from humble origins and then spread across the country and even around the world. In this chapter, we will read about some of the musical styles that American musicians have created.

> **"**True music must repeat the thought and inspirations of the people and the time.**"**
>
> —George Gershwin,
> American composer

Overall Impressions

READING 1

Prereading

Before you read, discuss the following questions with your classmates.

1. What kind of music do you like? Why do you like it? Who has influenced your taste in music?

2. How are culture and music related?

3. This reading is about American music. Here is a list of some of the different types of American music that are mentioned in this article. Do you know any of these types of music?

bluegrass	blues	Cajun
country	disco	folk
funk	gospel and spiritual	hip-hop
jazz	pop	ragtime
rock-and-roll	soul	zydeco

Predicting

Predicting can help you understand what you read. Before you read, do the following activities. They will help you predict what the reading selection will be about.

1. Look at Chart 5.1. Do you recognize any of the names of the musicians? What do you know about these musicians?

2. Look at the words to the songs on pages 122 and 123. Have you ever heard these songs before? Can you sing them? How do you think the songs are related to the reading topic?

**Previewing
Specialized
Vocabulary**

Listed here are some of the specialized words that you will find in this reading selection. Knowing and understanding these words will help you understand the reading selection better.

- Review the definitions of these words.
- Identify which of these words, if any, you already know.
- Try to paraphrase the meaning of each word.
- Underline these words in the reading selection.

musicologist (*n.*)—a person who studies music (paragraph 1)

hymn (*n.*)—a religious song usually sung in church (paragraph 4)

melodies (*n.*)—organized sequences of tones that fit together to create a musical phrase or idea (paragraph 5)

harmonies (*n.*)—combinations of musical notes in chords (paragraph 5)

rhythms (*n.*)—patterns of musical movement (paragraph 5)

improvisation (*n.*)—playing music without following a preset composition (paragraph 5)

cross-fertilize (*v.*)—to exchange concepts between cultures, usually resulting in new ways of thinking (paragraph 5)

lyrics (*n.*)—the words to songs (paragraph 6)

racist (*adj.*)—holding prejudices based on race (paragraph 6)

cosmopolitan (*adj.*)—sophisticated, worldly (paragraph 7)

dance hall (*n. ph.*)—a place for dancing, similar to a nightclub or discotheque (paragraph 7)

revered (*adj.*)—held in esteem; regarded with devotion (paragraph 9)

rebellious (*adj.*)—resisting the control of others (paragraph 13)

American Music

Music and Culture

1   What can music tell us about a society? According to the musicologist Robert Santelli, American music is democratic. "It speaks to us in a common language. It connects us despite our cultural diversities. It sidesteps class and other social barriers[1]."

2   Music has played a significant role in the culture of the United States. During the twentieth century, American culture fostered[2] many forms of popular music. Americans of all backgrounds have contributed to the development of the nation's musical varieties. Regional, ethnic, and class differences have inspired[3] diverse musical styles. These styles include blues, ragtime, jazz, gospel, country and western, Cajun, bluegrass, zydeco, rock-and-roll, soul, funk, disco, and hip-hop. As Robert Santelli concludes, "America is a nation of beats and rhythms, a culture consumed by sound."

3   This rich musical tradition has had an important influence on American culture and values. Pop music affects what Americans wear, how they speak, and what they buy. Music has even helped shape what Americans think about politics, sex, and race relations.

---

[1]**social barriers** (*n. ph.*) — obstacles to interaction among different groups in society
[2]**to foster** (*v.*) — to promote the growth of
[3]**to inspire** (*v.*) — to help bring into existence

CHART 5.1   FAMOUS AMERICAN MUSIC MAKERS

Here are the names of some famous American music makers. How many do you recognize?

Stephen Foster	Aaron Copeland	Judy Garland
Scott Joplin	Woody Guthrie	Frank Sinatra
John Philip Sousa	Cole Porter	James Brown
Louis Armstrong	Billie Holliday	B. B. King
Duke Ellington	Benny Goodman	Chuck Berry
George Gershwin	Bing Crosby	John Coltrane
Irving Berlin	Charlie Parker	Pete Seeger
Jelly Roll Morton	Hank Williams	Bob Dylan
Richard Rodgers	Muddy Waters	Aretha Franklin
Bessie Smith	Miles Davis	Jimi Hendrix
The Carter Family	Elvis Presley	Paul Simon
Ella Fitzgerald	Marian Anderson	Tupac Shakur

History of Music in the United States

4   Until the middle of the nineteenth century, most music played in the United States originated in Europe. Classical music, folk music, and religious songs (hymns) came with colonists and immigrants from their countries. Sometimes these new Americans added their own words to familiar tunes. A famous example is the song "Yankee Doodle Dandy." During the American Revolution, British soldiers sang this song as a way of making fun of the American troops. But the American soldiers soon adopted the song and made up new words to celebrate their commander, George Washington. To this day, the song remains an American favorite, especially during Independence Day celebrations on the Fourth of July.

Yankee Doodle

VERSE 1

Yankee Doodle went to town
A-riding on a pony
Stuck a feather in his hat
And called it macaroni[4].

CHORUS

Yankee Doodle, keep it up
Yankee Doodle dandy
Mind the music and the step
And with the girls be handy.

---

[4]**macaroni** (*adj.*) — fashionable, elegant (*eighteenth-century slang*)

VERSE 2

There was Captain Washington
Upon a slapping stallion[5]
A-giving orders to his men
I guess there was a million.

CHORUS

Early Influence of African Americans

5   Europeans weren't the only people to bring a rich musical tradition from their homelands. African slaves kept alive the music of their native cultures. Their music was quite different from that of the Europeans. European music uses elaborate melodies and harmonies. In African music, complex rhythms are more important. These rhythms are often expressed through improvisation. By the end of the Civil War (1861–1865), these diverse traditions began to cross-fertilize each other. This led to the development of the unique styles that characterize modern American music. Robert Santelli suggests that the one thing that makes American music different from that of all other nations is the creative tension that comes from its black and white roots.

6   This creative tension informed the compositions of America's first famous songwriter. A white man from Pittsburgh, Pennsylvania, Stephen Foster borrowed from black music. His songs were extremely popular in the middle of the nineteenth century. However, the songs painted an overly romantic[6] picture of black life in the South. Foster visited the South only once. For this reason, some people question the accuracy of his songs. From today's more sensitive perspective, some of the lyrics seem racist. Nevertheless, Foster was the first American songwriter to gain widespread popularity. His songs are still familiar to Americans in the twenty-first century.

Oh! Susanna

VERSE 1

I come from Alabama with a banjo[7] on my knee.
I'm going to Louisiana, my true love for to see.
It rained all night the day I left; the weather it was dry.
Sun so hot I froze to death; Susanna, don't you cry.

CHORUS

Oh! Susanna, don't you cry for me.
I come from Alabama with a banjo on my knee.

VERSE 2

I had a dream the other night when everything was still.
I dreamed I saw Susanna way up on the hill.
Buckwheat cakes[8] was in her mouth, the tears was in her eyes.
Said I'm a coming from the south, Susanna, don't you cry.

▲ Stephen Foster

[5]**stallion** (*n.*) — an adult male horse
[6]**romantic** (*adj.*) — derived more from imagination than reality
[7]**banjo** (*n.*) — a stringed instrument of African origin
[8]**buckwheat cakes** (*n. ph.*) — pancakes made from buckwheat flour

CHORUS

VERSE 3

I'm headed down to New Orleans, and there I'll look around.
And if I do not find Susanna, I'll fall upon the ground.
And if I do not find her, then I'll surely die.
And when I'm dead and buried, Susanna, don't you cry.

CHORUS

The Rise of Distinctive American Styles

7   At the start of the twentieth century, the United States became a more cosmopolitan nation. For the first time, more people lived in cities than in rural areas. Millions of immigrants arrived. African Americans migrated north to cities like New York and Chicago. These cultural groups mixed together in the rapidly growing cities. American music also became more cosmopolitan at this time. Folk music, such as "hillbilly" music (now called country and western), found large audiences in Memphis, Chicago, Nashville, and New York. The integration of cultures encouraged musical experimentation and innovation. Suddenly, new musical styles began to grow. First ragtime and then jazz swept the dance halls of the nation.

Tin Pan Alley

8   New technology, such as radio and the phonograph, introduced more people to the emerging sounds. Music soon became a commercial product like other goods. To this day, Americans speak of the "music industry." The notion of a music industry had its origins in a section of Manhattan called Tin Pan Alley. Here, in the first decades of the twentieth century, songwriters, music publishers, and producers came together to write songs for musical theaters and radio shows. Irving Berlin and George Gershwin were two of the most famous songwriters of Tin Pan Alley.

9   Irving Berlin was born in Russia. As a young boy, he came to New York with his family. He could not read or write music. Nevertheless, he composed more than a thousand songs, including some that Americans have loved and cherished for generations, such as "Alexander's Ragtime Band," "White Christmas," and "There's No Business like Show Business." One Berlin song, "God Bless America," is particularly revered.

10   Like many other Tin Pan Alley songwriters, George Gershwin was the son of Jewish immigrants. A gifted pianist, Gershwin played both jazz and classical music. He wrote popular music, such as America's first successful opera (*Porgy and Bess*), as well as more sophisticated compositions, such as the much-admired "Rhapsody in Blue." He died of a brain tumor in 1937, when he was only thirty-nine years old.

11   Tin Pan Alley was the foundation for Broadway and Hollywood musicals, which continue to attract mass audiences. From *Show Boat* (which first opened on Broadway in 1927) to *Oklahoma!* (1943), *West Side Story* (1957), and *Chicago* (a movie hit in 2002), musicals on stage and screen have given Americans some of their favorite songs.

Jazz

12   From the 1920s to the 1940s, jazz was the most popular music in America. Jazz began in New Orleans early in the twentieth century. Jazz evolved from the work chants, spirituals, and folk music of African Americans. It reflects the rhythms and expressions of West African music. The first jazz bands featured cornets, trombones, and clarinets playing improvised melodies, while a piano, banjo, string bass, tuba, or drums provided the rhythm. These bands played in parades and dance halls. Soon jazz spread from New Orleans to Chicago, Kansas City, and New York. The heyday for jazz came in the 1930s and 1940s when "swing jazz" ruled the dance halls. Louis Armstrong and Duke Ellington were two of the biggest stars in jazz. Over time, jazz developed from a folk music of the South into a sophisticated modern art. In fact, many scholars claim that jazz is the most outstanding contribution the United States has made to world culture.

Rock-and-Roll

13   In the 1950s, a new form of music emerged on the scene and became popular the world over. Rock-and-roll, the new sound of American popular music, appealed to young people. It was rebellious. It celebrated life and sexual freedom. Rock-and-roll seemed to challenge established customs and rules of conduct. It represented independence and a new way of expressing oneself. The star of this new music was Elvis Presley. He was born in Tupelo, Mississippi, and moved to Memphis, Tennessee, when he was a teenager. In Memphis, he was immersed[9] in the sounds of both blues and country. Elvis was not the first to bring these sounds together. But he had a stage personality that seemed to represent everything rock-and-roll stood for. Although he grew up in poverty, Elvis became the most successful recording artist ever, the biggest star of the American music industry.

New Types of American Music

14   In the second half of the twentieth century, other types of music, including soul music and country music, shared the stage with rock-and-roll. Often these different types of music overlapped and influenced each other. Perhaps the most intriguing characteristic of American popular music is the many diverse styles that have influenced it. The United States is a nation of people who come from somewhere else, and the nation's diverse music is one obvious expression of this variety.

---

[9]**immersed** (*adj.*) — enveloped as if completely surrounded

READING SKILLS

EXERCISE 1   **Finding the Main Idea**

Review the reading again. Match each paragraph or group of paragraphs with the main idea. The first one has been done for you as an example.

a. Paragraphs 1–3   e. Paragraph 7   i. Paragraph 11
b. Paragraph 4   f. Paragraph 8   j. Paragraph 12
c. Paragraph 5   g. Paragraph 9   k. Paragraph 13
d. Paragraph 6   h. Paragraph 10   l. Paragraph 14

__d__   **1.** Stephen Foster borrowed from the African music tradition.

_____   **2.** Jazz developed from the traditional music of African Americans.

_____   **3.** As the United States became more urban, distinct styles of music began to develop.

_____   **4.** Rock-and-roll music represented independence and rebellion; it challenged established customs.

_____   **5.** Music in the United States is democratic and has had an important influence on American culture and values.

_____   **6.** The music industry developed because radio and phonographs were available to more people.

_____   **7.** George Gershwin wrote both popular and classical music.

_____   **8.** The United States has a wide variety of music because of the diversity of its people.

_____   **9.** In the beginning, most music in the United States was adapted from European music.

_____ **10.** Musical theater in Broadway and Hollywood has its roots in Tin Pan Alley.

_____ **11.** Irving Berlin was a prolific songwriter.

_____ **12.** African American slaves contributed complex rhythms to American music.

EXERCISE 2   **Acknowledging the Ideas of Others**

Academic texts often use the words or ideas of scholars. To make it clear that an idea is from another person, the text will use special words or phrases. Some examples of these special words or phrases are printed in bold letters in this exercise. Find the words or phrases in the reading selection. Then complete the statement here. The first one has been done for you as an example.

1. (Paragraph 1) **According to** the musicologist Robert Santelli,

   American music is democratic. "It speaks to us in a common

   language. It connects us despite our cultural diversities. It

   sidesteps class and other social barriers."

2. (Paragraph 2) As Robert Santelli **concludes**, ————————

————————————————————————

————————————————————————

3. (Paragraph 5) Robert Santelli **suggests that** ——————

————————————————————————

————————————————————————

4. (Paragraph 12) In fact, many scholars **claim** ——————

————————————————————————

———— ——————————————

EXERCISE 3   **Using Headings to Remember Details**

In academic settings, you will often be tested on reading selections. One way to remember what you have read is to copy the headings of the different sections of a reading selection and write notes on as many details as you can remember. Under each section in this exercise:

- Write short notes about what you remember from each section of the reading selection.

- Share what you wrote with a partner.
- Add any details from your partner's notes that you might have missed.
- Go back to the reading selection. Check to make sure your notes are correct. Add any details that you might have missed.

Music and Culture

History of Music in the United States

Early Influence of African Americans

The Rise of Distinctive American Styles

   Tin Pan Alley

   Jazz

   Rock-and-Roll

   New Types of American Music

VOCABULARY SKILLS

EXERCISE 4

Academic Word List

The following words are frequently found in academic writing. Knowing these words will help you read all kinds of academic texts. The first list is of Academic Words that you have seen earlier in this book. You can find these words again in this reading selection. Make sure these words are in your vocabulary notebook. (See page 7 for information about how to make a vocabulary notebook.) Add any new information that you learn about these words to your vocabulary notebook. The number in parentheses indicates the paragraph in this reading selection where the word appears.

1. despite (1)
2. cultural (1), culture (2)
3. role (2)
4. contributed (2)
5. regional (2)
6. diverse (2)

7. tradition (3)
8. affects (3)
9. immigrants (4)
10. creative (5)
11. unique (5)
12. civil (5)
13. widespread (6)

14. technology (8)
15. emerging (8)
16. publisher (8)
17. decades (8)
18. generations (9)
19. foundation (11)
20. featured (12)

The second list is of Academic Words that are new in this reading selection. Add these words to your vocabulary notebook. The number in parentheses indicates the paragraph in this reading selection where the word appears.

1. significant (2)
2. ethnic (2)
3. styles (2)
4. concludes (2)
5. consumed (2)
6. sex (3), sexual (13)
7. classical (4)

8. revolution (4)
9. tension (5)
10. perspective (6)
11. nevertheless (6)
12. migrated (7)
13. integration (7)
14. notion (8)
15. section (8)

16. evolved (12)
17. contribution (12)
18. challenge (13)
19. established (13)
20. conduct (13)
21. overlap (14)
22. obvious (14)

EXERCISE 5

Improving Dictionary Skills

Some words are spelled the same in their noun or verb forms. Sometimes the words change meaning in their verb and noun forms, and sometimes they change pronunciation. Ask your teacher to pronounce the words for you.

- Use a dictionary to find the following words.
- Write a sentence with the noun and verb forms of the words.
- Read the sentence from the reading selection. Decide if each word is a noun or verb.

The first one has been done for you as an example.

1. conduct (*n.*) *The students who are polite have good conduct.*

   conduct (*v.*) *You must conduct a research study.*

   Rock-and-roll seemed to challenge established customs and rules of **conduct**. *noun*

2. challenge (*n.*) _____

   challenge (*v.*) _____

   Rock-and-roll seemed to **challenge** established customs and rules of conduct. _____

3. feature (*n.*) _____

   feature (*v.*) _____

   The first jazz bands **featured** cornets, trombones, and clarinets playing improvised melodies, while a piano, banjo, string bass, tuba, or drums provided the rhythm. _____

4. style (*n.*) _____

   style (*v.*) _____

   Regional, ethnic, and class differences have inspired such diverse musical **styles**. _____

5. buy (*v.*) _____

   buy (*n.*) _____

   Pop music affects what Americans wear, how they speak, and what they **buy**. _____

6. shape (*n.*) _____

   shape (*v.*) _____

Music has even helped **shape** what Americans think about politics, sex, and race relations. _____

7. remains (*n.*) _____

remains (*v.*) _____

To this day, the song **remains** an American favorite, especially during Independence Day celebrations on the Fourth of July.

_____

EXERCISE 6

Collocations with Adverbs

Adverbs can describe verbs. Most verbs in English are found with certain adverbs. When words are written together often, we call them *collocations*. For example, the adverb *greatly* is often found before the verb *affect*. One way to improve your vocabulary is to notice the words that are often found together.

Here are some of the adverbs that are commonly found with some of the Academic Words from this reading selection. Study the chart, answer the questions, and do the activities.

1. What do all the following adverbs have in common?

2. What words are often found with *seriously*?

3. What words are often found with *successfully*?

4. What words have the same meaning as *successfully challenge*?

5. What words have the same meaning as *thoroughly integrate*?

6. Say the adverbs together with the verbs. This will help you remember which adverbs and verbs go together.

7. Write one sentence with each of the verbs and an adverb that goes with it.

Adverb	Academic Words This Adverb Can Modify
adversely	affect
completely	emerge, integrate
directly	affect, challenge
effectively	challenge, integrate
finally	emerge
greatly	affect
independently	conduct
personally	conduct
prominently	feature

Adverb	Academic Words This Adverb Can Modify
regularly	conduct, feature
seriously	affect, challenge
significantly	affect
slowly	emerge
strongly	affect, challenge
successfully	affect, conduct, integrate
suddenly	emerge
thoroughly	integrate

DISCUSSION ACTIVITIES

Form a group of three or four students. Review the rules for group work your class created in the activity on page 10. Do one of the following activities.

1. Use research materials, such as an encyclopedia, to find additional information about one of the musicians or groups listed in Chart 5.1. Share what you have learned with your other classmates.

2. What kind of music do you like? Bring a sample of music from your favorite artist to class to share with your group members. Tell your group members about the artist. Explain why you like that kind of music.

READING-RESPONSE JOURNAL

Choose one of the following topics, and write about it in your journal.

1. Describe one thing you learned about American music that you did not know before you read this selection.

2. What are two topics that you read about in this selection that you would like to know more information about. Explain why those two topics are especially interesting to you.

WRITING TOPICS

Choose one of the following topics, and write a composition.

1. Robert Santelli says that American music "connects us despite our cultural diversities. It sidesteps class and other social barriers." Do you think music in the United States has a unifying effect, as Santelli says, or do different kinds of music divide people by culture and class? Support your opinion with examples from your experiences and what you have read about American music.

2. Choose one American value from Chapter 1, and explain how American music expresses that value.

3. The commercial aspects of American culture have spread around the world, including American movies, American music, American products, and American television. Are you familiar with another country or culture that has been influenced by the United States? Has this influence been mostly positive or mostly negative? Use specific examples to explain your point of view. The essay that follows in "Student Impressions" is an example of one response to this question.

4. American music has been influenced by many different types of music. Describe your favorite type of music. How has it been influenced by other cultures? Do you think this outside influence is positive or negative?

STUDENT IMPRESSIONS

In the following essay, a student from the Dominican Republic writes about the influence of American pop music in her homeland.

Traditional Music Is Best

The traditional music of my country is called *merengue*. In its original form, this music had a simple style using common instruments like the accordion and saxophone. Often these instruments, like the drums, were homemade. *Merengue* was popular in the countryside and later became popular in the cities. When I was a girl, the *meringue* bands played at all the festivals and dances. Everybody loved this national music, and you heard it everywhere.

Nowadays when I go back to visit my country, it is still possible to hear *merengue* music, but even more I hear the American songs everywhere. Wherever I go, I hear popular music from the United States. The young people now like Britney Spears, Michael Jackson, and Madonna more than the traditional music of their country. This makes me very sad, because I think the singers of this music do not have good morality. Also, the singers represent a culture very different from our traditional culture. The young people want to be like Britney Spears, and this is not good.

Also, I think the English in these popular American songs is not so good. The singers use bad words and a lot of slang. It's not good for people to learn English from these songs. I wish the people in my country could be more interested in the traditional culture and music, but instead they want to imitate the American culture. Even our national music, *merengue*, has changed because of American music. Now you hear more computer sounds and electric guitars, which are not part of the traditional music. I guess the *merengue* musicians want to be like Britney Spears and Michael Jackson, too. I admit sometimes I like the American music. For example, I like Whitney Houston. There is a time and place for this music. But in my opinion, a festival in the Dominican Republic has to play only Dominican music, and that music is *merengue*.

In-Depth Impressions

READING 2

Prereading

Before you read, discuss the following questions with your classmates.

1. Have you ever heard of rap music? What do you already know about rap? What do you think about rap?

2. What kinds of clothes and fashions are associated with hip-hop culture?

Predicting

Before you read, do the following activities. They will help you predict what the reading selection will be about.

1. Look at the photo that goes with this reading selection. What are your impressions of the people in the photo? Share your impressions with your classmates.

2. In the first paragraph, you find out that hip-hop culture started in the 1970s and came from Caribbean and African cultural traditions. From these two facts, what can you predict about the characteristics of hip-hop culture?

Previewing Specialized Vocabulary

Listed here are some of the specialized words that you will find in this reading selection. Knowing and understanding these words will help you understand the reading selection better.

- Review the definitions of these words.
- Identify which of these words, if any, you already know.
- Try to paraphrase the meaning of each word.
- Underline these words in the reading selection.

urban (*adj.*)—related to or characteristic of a city (paragraph 1)

rhythmic (*adj.*)—having rhythm (paragraph 2)

rhyming (*adj.*)—using words with identical terminal sounds (paragraph 2)

graffiti (*n.*)—drawings or inscriptions on walls (paragraph 2)

folk hero (*n.*)—a heroic character in folklore (paragraph 3)

mainstream (*adj.*)—related to the dominant ideas or values of a group or a society (paragraph 5)

misogynistic (*adj.*)—displaying hatred or disrespect for women (paragraph 6)

gangster (*n.*)—member of an organized group of criminals (paragraph 7)

entrepreneurship (*n.*)—running a business (paragraph 8)

The Emergence of Hip-Hop

1   *Hip-hop* is the name of a cultural movement originating in the United States. Although it developed in North America, its roots can be traced to Caribbean and African cultural traditions. Aspects of hip-hop culture first appeared in urban areas of the United States during the 1970s. At first, it was popular in inner-city areas, such as the South Bronx in New York City. Then, during the 1980s and 1990s, it attained national fame and worldwide popularity.

2   The most widely recognized component of hip-hop culture is rap. Rap is a musical style that uses rhythmic, rhyming speech. Sometimes the terms *rap* and *hip-hop* are used as synonyms, but in actuality, rap is only one aspect of the complex culture of hip-hop. Other cultural components associated with hip-hop have included deejaying (the skillful manipulation of a turntable to create interesting rhythmic effects); graffiti painting, or "tagging" of walls and subway cars; dance styles such as break dancing; distinctive fashions; and a set of overtly masculine gestures and mannerisms sometimes referred to as "B-boying."

The History of Rap Music

3   A young Jamaican immigrant named Clive Campbell is sometimes credited with inventing rap. Using the name DJ Kool Herc, Campbell became known for speaking in clever rhyming patterns as he played records. But Campbell's speaking style had many forerunners in African, Caribbean, and African American cultures. Rap is similar to West African storytelling. It is also like the Jamaican tradition of "toasting," a rhythmic speech before an audience. "Talking blues" songs and long, rhyming poems of folk heroes are also part of rap's roots.

4   The major pioneers of rap music include the artists Grandmaster Flash and Afrika Bambaataa. The first rap record to achieve national popularity, however,

▲ Run-D.M.C

was "Rapper's Delight" by the Sugarhill Gang. Soon after its release in 1979, it became one of the most popular records in the United States. Across the country, young people learned a new term and a new musical style: rap.

5   The success of "Rapper's Delight" paved the way for the top stars of the 1980s. Perhaps the most popular and influential act was Run-D.M.C., three middle-class African American men from New York. Combining rap with rock music, Run-D.M.C. reached a broad, mainstream audience. They also introduced new fashions to a youth culture eager for distinctive trends. Other popular artists of the time included LL Cool J, who gave rap a romantic flavor, and the Beastie Boys, the first successful white rap group.

The Popularization of Rap

6　　As rap became more popular, the music lost some of its original focus. Early artists, such as Grandmaster Flash, focused on politics and sang about social problems. During the 1980s, some artists continued this tradition. Public Enemy, for example, sang about political and social problems. Other artists, however, were content to focus on partying and male-female relationships—often presenting a misogynistic viewpoint. Some social commentators criticized this trend in hip-hop culture.

7　　In the early 1990s, a new variety of rap developed on the West Coast, primarily in the Compton district of Los Angeles. This style of rap was called "gangsta rap" because the music glorified gangster behavior. It soon became notorious for its graphic and violent lyrics. Artists such as Ice-T, Snoop Doggy Dogg, Dr. Dre, and Tupac Shakur said that their music told the truth about life in the inner cities of America. They claimed that their lyrics described violence because that was the reality they had experienced in their neighborhoods. Defenders of gangsta rap said that racism and poverty were the real causes of urban violence. Rap music, they claimed, was the best way for the victims of racism and poverty to tell America what was really happening.

8　　By the year 2000, new artists such as Wu-Tang Clan, Puff Daddy, the Fugees, Eminem, and OutKast had made rap the best-selling music in the United Sates. Hip-hop culture was also responsible for popularizing numerous products. The clothing, shoes, cars, and liquor favored by rap artists in their videos became popular with young people all over the world. Hip-hop had entered a new phase. It had once been fashionable only for the underclass. Now it was a dynamic blend of art and entrepreneurship, responsible for more than $1 billion in music sales each year and more than $2 billion in clothing sales.

READING SKILLS

EXERCISE 7　　**Finding the Main Idea**

Read the following sentences. If the sentence is the main idea of the paragraph in the reading selection, write *MI* in the blank in front of the sentence. If it is a detail from the paragraph, write *D*, and then write the main idea in your own words. The first one has been done for you as an example.

　D　**1.** Aspects of hip-hop culture first appeared during the 1970s.

　　Hip-hop is a cultural movement from the United States

　　that grew from Caribbean and African roots.

　_____　**2.** Rap music is the most widely recognized component of hip-hop.

　　_____

　　_____

_____ **3.** Clive Campbell used the name DJ Kool Herc.

_____

_____

_____ **4.** "Rapper's Delight" made rap music popular.

_____

_____

_____ **5.** Run-D.M.C. popularized rap music and fashion.

_____

_____

_____ **6.** Rap music became misogynistic.

_____

_____

_____ **7.** Gangsta rap glorified violence, but defenders said that it was a voice for victims of racism and poverty.

_____

_____

_____ **8.** By 2000, hip-hop culture was mainstream big business.

_____

_____

EXERCISE 8

Answering Comprehension Questions

One way to find specific information in a reading passage is called _skimming_. Skimming means that you do not have to read the whole passage. You look at the passage for key words in the question. When you find the key words, you look for the specific answer to the question. Use this technique to answer the following questions.

1. Where did hip-hop culture begin?

2. What are five components associated with hip-hop culture?

3. How was rap music influenced by West African culture?

4. How was rap music influenced by Jamaican culture?

5. Who recorded "Rapper's Delight"?

6. What was the first successful white rap group?

7. Which two rap artists focused on politics and social problems?

8. What type of rap music are Ice-T, Snoop Doggy Dogg, Dr. Dre, and Tupac Shakur known for?

9. What are three types of products influenced by hip-hop culture?

VOCABULARY SKILLS

EXERCISE 9

Academic Word List

The following words are frequently found in academic writing. Knowing these words will help you read all kinds of academic texts. The first list is of Academic Words that you have seen earlier in this book. You can find these words again in this reading selection. Make sure these words are in your vocabulary notebook. (See page 7 for information about how to make a vocabulary notebook.) Add any new information that you learn about these words to your vocabulary notebook. The number in parentheses indicates the paragraph in this reading selection where the word appears.

1. cultural (1),
   culture (1)
2. traced (1)
3. traditions (1)
4. aspects (1)
5. areas (1)
6. complex (2)
7. distinctive (3)
8. immigrant (4)

The second list is of Academic Words that are new in this reading selection. Add these words to your vocabulary notebook. The number in parentheses indicates the paragraph in this reading selection where the word appears.

1. attained (1)
2. style (2)
3. components (2)
4. manipulation (2)
5. credited (3)
6. trend (5)
7. phase (8)
8. dynamic (8)

EXERCISE 10

Learning Academic Words

Do the following activities to learn the Academic Words.

1. Look over the list of words.

2. Circle the words that you already know.

3. Work with a partner. Compare the words you know with the words your partner knows. Help each other learn words.

4. Look at the Academic Words that you still do not know. Create a graphic organizer for at least five words that you want to learn well. Use a dictionary to help you find the information you do not know.

Each graphic organizer should have the following parts:

- Synonyms of the word
- Related word forms
- Words commonly found with that word (collocations)
- Example sentence or phrase

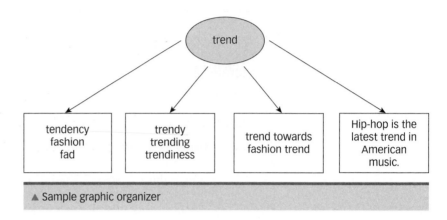

▲ Sample graphic organizer

EXERCISE **11**   **Using Context Clues**

Many times you can determine the meaning of a word from the other words in the sentence. Look at each of the following words. Using the other words in the sentence, write a definition for each word.

1. **roots** (paragraph 1): *Hip-hop* is the name of a cultural movement originating in the United States. Although it developed in North America, its **roots** can be traced to Caribbean and African cultural traditions. *beginning* _____

2. **rap** (paragraph 2): **Rap** is a musical style that uses rhythmic, rhyming speech. _____

3. **deejaying** (paragraph 2): Other cultural components associated with hip-hop have included **deejaying** (the skillful manipulation of a turntable to create interesting rhythmic effects) . . .

_____

4. **tagging** (paragraph 2): . . . graffiti painting, or "**tagging**" of walls and subway cars, . . . _____

5. **B-boying** (paragraph 2): . . . a set of overtly masculine gestures and mannerisms sometimes referred to as "**B-boying.**" _____

_____

6. **forerunners** (paragraph 3): But Campbell's speaking style had many **forerunners** in African, Caribbean, and African American cultures.

_____

7. **toasting** (paragraph 3): It is also like the Jamaican tradition of "**toasting**," a rhythmic speech before an audience. _____

_____

8. **paved the way** (paragraph 5): The success of "Rapper's Delight" **paved the way** for the top stars of the 1980s. _____

_____

9. **gangsta rap** (paragraph 7): This style of rap was called "**gangsta rap**" because the music glorified gangster behavior. _____

_____

DISCUSSION ACTIVITIES

Form a group of three or four students. Review the rules for group work your class created in the activity on page 10. Discuss the following topics. Report to your classmates what your group talked about.

1. Rap music, especially gangsta rap, has been criticized because it focuses on violence. What do rappers say to their critics? Who do you think is correct, the rappers or their critics? Defend your answer.

2. Do you like rap music? Explain why you like it or not.

READING-RESPONSE JOURNAL

Choose one of the following topics, and write about it in your journal.

1. What did you learn from your reading that you did not know before? What surprised you? Explain why it surprised you.

2. Was this reading selection mostly written for fans of hip-hop culture or people who do not know much about hip-hop? What in the reading selection tells you that it was written for that group?

WRITING TOPICS

Choose one of the following topics, and write a composition.

1. Rap has influenced music in the United States and in countries around the world. Describe a fashion, type of music, or other cultural item that has had influence around the world.

2. Hip-hop culture has influenced mainstream culture in the United States. What evidence do you see of this on TV, in advertising, and in the products that young people buy? Describe at least two examples of how hip-hop has influenced U.S. culture.

Personal Impressions

READING 3

Prereading

Before you read, discuss the following questions with your classmates.

1. Have you ever heard of Louis Armstrong? What do you know about him?

2. What do you remember about jazz music from Reading 1?

Predicting

Before you read, do the following activities. They will help you predict what the reading selection will be about.

1. Look at the photo of Louis Armstrong. What kind of person do you think he was?

2. The subtitle of this reading selection is "America's Musical Ambassador." What do you think this means?

Previewing Specialized Vocabulary

Listed here are some of the specialized words that you will find in this reading selection. Knowing and understanding these words will help you understand the reading selection better.

- Review the definitions of these words.
- Identify which of these words, if any, you already know.
- Try to paraphrase the meaning of each word.
- Underline these words in the reading selection.

ambassador (*n.*)—a representative, usually of a country (paragraph 1)

mourned (*v.*)—felt sorrow, grieved (paragraph 1)

pay tribute (*v. ph.*)—to give respect (paragraph 1)

gravestone (*n.*)—a stone used to mark a grave (paragraph 2)

reform school (*n. ph.*)—a school for children who have broken laws (paragraph 2)

impromptu (*adj.*)—done or put together without advanced planning (paragraph 3)

nonsensical (*adj.*)—without meaning (paragraph 6)

crisscrossed (*v.*)—traveled back and forth (paragraph 7)

prevalent (*adj.*)—typical, common (paragraph 9)

Louis Armstrong: America's Musical Ambassador

▲ Louis Armstrong

1   When Louis Armstrong died in 1971, millions of music lovers around the world mourned his death. More than twenty thousand people attended his funeral, an event so important it was broadcast on television. Everyone wanted to pay tribute to the man who was universally acknowledged as the greatest and most popular jazz musician of all time.

2   Although he was world-famous at the end of his life, Armstrong grew up in poverty. Born in 1901, he was raised in a poor section of New Orleans called "The Battlefield." Poverty and racism made his early years difficult. From the time he was a small boy, he had to work hard. He did odd jobs, such as selling newspapers, unloading boats, hauling coal in a cart, and cleaning gravestones. He also earned pennies by singing songs on street corners. Once he got in trouble for shooting a gun during New Year's celebrations. He was sent to a reform school for African American boys, where he remained until he was fourteen.

3   At the beginning of the twentieth century, New Orleans provided a rich environment for a young, musically inclined person. The music of the city inspired young Louis's natural genius. He heard blues musicians playing on the streets of Storyville, an African American section of New Orleans. He heard brass bands playing in dance halls, in parades, and at funerals. Intrigued by these bands, he taught himself to play the cornet. Soon he was good enough to perform with impromptu bands in clubs and parades. The best trumpet player in New Orleans, King Oliver, heard Louis playing and was impressed by the boy's natural talent. King Oliver became Louis's mentor and taught him the tricks of the trade.

4   In 1919, King Oliver left New Orleans for Chicago, where jazz was gaining in popularity. For a while, the teenaged Louis played with bands on the riverboats that traveled the Mississippi River. Then, in 1922, he received a message from King Oliver. Louis's mentor wanted the young man to join him in Chicago. This was a dream come true for Armstrong. Once he arrived in Chicago, Armstrong was an overnight sensation. His inspired performances took the town by storm. People marveled at his innovative technique and his brilliant solos. Almost single-handedly, Armstrong was transforming jazz from dance music into an art form.

5   Next, Armstrong took his music to New York. His arrival in the city coincided with an energetic artistic movement in Harlem, a large African American neighborhood in Manhattan. This movement, known as the Harlem Renaissance, featured a remarkable flourishing[10] in African American literature, music, dance, and visual arts. Armstrong's music provided a vibrant soundtrack for both the Harlem Renaissance and the so-called Jazz Age, a term used to describe the fast pace of cultural, social, and economic life in the America of the 1920s.

---

[10]**flourishing** (*n.*) — experiencing a burst in creativity and productivity

6   Now the leader of his own band, Armstrong made numerous records. The recordings of Louis Armstrong's Hot Five (they later became the Hot Seven) are considered jazz classics. Many jazz experts think "West End Blues" (1928) is Armstrong's greatest masterpiece. He also recorded a song called "Heebie Jeebies," which introduced Armstrong's unique style of singing to a wide audience. Known as "scat singing," this style calls for the singer to use nonsensical phrases. In effect, the singer's voice becomes a musical instrument. To this day, no one has had a more recognizable singing voice than Louis Armstrong.

7   For the rest of his life, Armstrong and his band toured extensively. He criss-crossed the United States, introducing his music to more and more people. Then Armstrong traveled to Europe, where he won over audiences in Denmark, Sweden, Norway, the Netherlands, France, and England. He performed in films, on radio, and in theaters, dance halls, and nightclubs. He became the most famous musician in the world, one of the great international celebrities of the twentieth century. Huge crowds came out to hear his band, the Louis Armstrong All-Stars, in Asia, South America, and Africa. During one trip to West Africa, 100,000 people greeted his arrival. The whole world knew him by his lifelong nickname, Satchmo (derived from "satchel mouth," a reference to his wide, ever-present smile).

8   Armstrong won the hearts of people everywhere. He had an unassuming, easy-going manner. His broad grin, quick wit, and positive outlook made people feel good. His international renown earned him the title of "America's Ambassador," or simply "Ambassador Satch." In the last decade of his career, still at the peak of his popularity, Armstrong recorded songs such as "Hello, Dolly!" which bumped the Beatles from the top of the pop charts in 1964, and "What a Wonderful World," which became a hit seventeen years after his death and remains popular today.

9   Without question, Louis Armstrong was a great human being. He rose out of poverty, confronted and overcame the racism that was prevalent in the United States at the time, and forever changed the world of music. As an artist, his influence continues to this day. Simply put, he is the most important figure in jazz history.

READING SKILLS

EXERCISE 12   **Finding the Main Idea**

Write the main idea of each paragraph. The first one has been done for you as an example.

1. (Paragraph 1) _Louis Armstrong is considered the greatest_
   and most popular jazz musician of all time.

2. (Paragraph 2) _____

3. (Paragraph 3) _____

4. (Paragraph 4) _____

5. (Paragraph 5) _____

6. (Paragraph 6) _____

7. (Paragraph 7) _____

8. (Paragraph 8) _____

9. (Paragraph 9) _____

EXERCISE 13 **Sequencing Details**

Here are some details from Louis Armstrong's life. Review the reading selection. Number the details in the order in which they occurred in his life. Detail number one has been done for you as an example.

_____ As a small boy, Louis Armstrong had to work.

_____ Louis Armstrong went to Chicago to join King Oliver.

_____ Louis Armstrong toured Europe.

_____ "Hello, Dolly!" was more popular than the Beatles on the pop charts.

_____ Louis Armstrong died.

_____ Louis Armstrong moved to New York.

_____ Louis Armstrong recorded "West End Blues."

_1_ Louis Armstrong was born in New Orleans.

_____ Louis Armstrong played with bands on riverboats as they cruised the Mississippi.

_____ Louis Armstrong was sent to reform school.

VOCABULARY SKILLS

EXERCISE 14 **Academic Word List**

The following words are frequently found in academic writing. Knowing these words will help you read all kinds of academic texts. The first list is of Academic Words that you have seen earlier in this book. You can find these words again in this reading selection. Make sure these words are in your vocabulary notebook. (See page 7 for information about how to make a vocabulary notebook.) Add any new information that you learn about these words to your vocabulary notebook. The number in parentheses indicates the paragraph in this reading selection where the word appears.

1. section (2)   **3.** energetic (5)   **5.** positive (8)

2. innovative (4)   **4.** economic (5)

The second list is of Academic Words that are new in this reading selection. Add these words to your vocabulary notebook. The number in parentheses indicates the paragraph in this reading selection where the word appears.

1. acknowledged (1)   **4.** coincided (5)   **7.** experts (6)

2. technique (4)   **5.** visual (5)   **8.** charts (8)

3. transforming (4)   **6.** classics (6)

EXERCISE **15** **Learning Academic Words**

Choose the correct Academic Word to complete each of the following sentences.

1. In some cities, there is a clear boundary between the poor _____ and the wealthy area.

2. Louis Armstrong developed an original and _____ style of singing.

3. The politician _____ that he had made a mistake.

4. A good musician must learn the proper _____ for playing an instrument.

5. Labor unions were important in _____ the working conditions in factories.

6. Their vacation in New Orleans _____ with the celebration of Mardi Gras.

7. The audience applauded the dancer's _____ performance.

8. Tourism can have a positive _____ impact on a city.

9. Louis Armstrong recorded many songs that are _____ of jazz.

10. Before remodeling her house, Carmen spoke to some _____.

11. Because of Harry's _____ outlook on life, his friends call him "Happy Harry."

12. A song that lots of people are downloading will rank high on the pop _____.

EXERCISE **16** **Idiomatic Phrases**

Idiomatic phrases are groups of words that have a special meaning when used together. Find each of the idiomatic phrases listed here in the reading selection. Match the phrase to its meaning. Phrase number one has been done for you as an example.

1. pay tribute (1)   5. overnight sensation (4)

2. odd jobs (2)   6. took the town by storm (4)

3. tricks of the trade (3)   7. won the hearts (8)

4. dream come true (4)   8. peak of his popularity (8)

_____ **a.** immediate success

_____ **b.** at a high point in one's career

__1__ **c.** to praise and honor

_____ **d.** small tasks done for a little money

_____ **e.** became popular and loved

_____ **f.** gained sudden fame and popularity

_____ **g.** a wish that became a reality

_____ **h.** clever, quick, or skillful ways of doing things

DISCUSSION ACTIVITIES

Form a group of three or four students. Review the rules for group work your class created in the activity on page 10. Discuss the following topics. Report to your classmates what your group talked about.

1. Often the personality and talent of one individual can make a musical style universally popular. Besides Louis Armstrong, can you think of any other musicians who have accomplished this?

2. Great artists often come from poor or disadvantaged backgrounds. Why do you think this happens? With your group members, list reasons why this might be true.

READING-RESPONSE JOURNAL

Choose one of the following topics, and write about it in your journal.

1. What kind of person was Louis Armstrong? What examples does the author give to show what kind of person he was?

2. What is the thing that most impressed you about the life of Louis Armstrong? Why did it impress you?

WRITING TOPICS

Choose one of the following topics, and write a composition.

1. One of the reasons why Louis Armstrong is considered a great human being is that he overcame racism and poverty to become one

of the best-known and most admired musicians in the world. Describe a person you know or have heard about who had to overcome great difficulties to be successful in life.

2. Louis Armstrong had natural talent as a musician. Which do you think is more important to success, talent or hard work? Give an example of an outstanding musician, athlete, or entertainer to illustrate your opinion.

INTERNET ACTIVITIES

For additional internet activities, go to **elt.thomson.com/impressions**

Credits

TEXT

Page 3: L. Robert Kohls, "The Values Americans Live By," available at numerous sites on web, including, www.uri.edu/mind/VALUES2.pdf

Page 23: From *John Muir: A Brief Biography* www.sierraclub.org/john_muir_ exhibit/life/muir_biography.html. Reproduced with permission from Sierra Club National Headquarters.

Page 75: From Mark Roberge, "California's Generation 1.5 Immigrants," *The CATESOL Journal* 14.1, 2002, pp. 107–129. Reprinted with permission of Mark Roberge, Editor, *CATESOL Journal* and Assistant Professor, San Francisco State University.

Page 85: Excerpt from Stephen Benz, "The Miracle Worker," *Tropic, The Miami Herald Sunday Magazine*, April 14, 1996. Copyright © 1996 by Miami Herald. Reproduced with permission of Miami Herald via Copyright Clearance Center.

Page 93: "This Land Is Your Land," words and music by Woody Guthrie. TRO-© Copyright 1956, (renewed) 1958, (renewed) 1970, (renewed) 1972, (renewed) Ludlow Music, Inc. New York, NY. Used by permission.

Pages 96–97: Illustration by Alexander Verbitsky. Reprinted with permission of McDougal Littell, a division of Houghton Mifflin.

Page 106: Adapted from *The Enduring Vision: A History of the American People*, by Paul S. Boyer, et al., pp. 497–501, 2000. Reprinted with permission of Houghton Mifflin Company.

Page 113: Excerpt from Stephen Benz, "The Long Road to Christmas," *Tropic, The Miami Herald Sunday Magazine*, December 7, 1997. Copyright © 1997 by Miami Herald. Reproduced with permission of Miami Herald via Copyright Clearance Center.

Page 121: Reprinted with permission of the National Geographic Society from the book *Defining a Nation* by David Halberstam. Copyright © 2003 Tahiti Books. Essay copyright © 2003 Robert Santelli.

PHOTOS

Page 1: © Jeff Greenberg/PhotoEdit

Page 14: left, © Hulton Archive/Getty Images; *right,* © MGM/CORBIS

Page 23: © CORBIS

Page 24: © E. O. Hoppé/CORBIS

Page 26: © Bettmann/CORBIS

Page 31: © Randy Faris/CORBIS

Page 34: top left, © Keystone/Getty Images; *top right,* © Bettmann/CORBIS; *bottom left,* © Peter Kramer/Getty Images; *bottom right,* © Eric Draper/CNP/CORBIS

Page 35: © Jeff Greenberg/The Image Works

Page 45: © Bettmann/CORBIS

Page 52: The Granger Collection, New York

Page 59: © Brooks Kraft/CORBIS

Page 62: AP Images

Page 63: © Mary Evans Picture Library/The Image Works

Page 64: © B. Newman/Three Lions/Getty Images

Page 75: © Bob Daemmrich/The Image Works

Page 76: © PhotoDisc/Getty Images

Page 77: © Aristide Economopoulos/Star Ledger/CORBIS

Page 93: © Ronnie Kaufman/CORBIS

Page 95: © Tom Bean/Getty Images

Page 106: © Lucidio Studio Inc./CORBIS

Page 107: The Granger Collection, New York

Page 119: © Nick White/Getty Images

Page 122: © CORBIS

Page 123: © Bettmann/CORBIS

Page 134: © Lynn Goldsmith/CORBIS

Page 142: © Bettmann/ CORBIS

Vocabulary Index

The list below includes all the words from the Academic Word List sections of the book.

accurate, 27 — *EXACTO - ACERTADO*
achieve, 17 — *ALCANZAR - REALIZAR*
acknowledged, 145
acquired, 38, 81 — *ADQUIRIR.*
adapt, 80 — *ADAPT*
adaptation, 80 — *ADAPTACIÓN*
adapting, 80
adjust, 81 — *Modificar, AJUSTAR.*
adjustment, 81 — *Modificación. AJUSTE.*
adults, 17
affect, 69 — *AFFECTAR - INFLUIR*
affected, 100
affects, 128
analysis, 7
analysts, 69
apparent, 115
appreciate, 48
approached, 115 — *ACERCARSE.*
area, 69, 109
areas, 137
aspect, 38
aspects, 99, 137
assignment, 89 — *ASIGNACIÓN - TAREA.*
assist, 81
assistant, 89
assumptions, 7 — *SUPOSICIÓN, PRESUNCIÓN*
attained, 137 — *ALCANZA - CONSEGUIR - LOGRAS*
attitudes, 100 — *ACTITUD - DISPOSICIÓN*
available, 89, 100 — *DISPONIBLE.*
benefits, 89, 109
categories, 80
category, 48, 80
challenge, 128 — *DESAFÍO RETO.*
chart, 7
charts, 145
civil, 100, 128
classical, 128
classics, 145
coincided, 145
comment, 115
commission, 89
commodities, 89
communities, 37, 68

community, 17, 89
complex, 109, 137
components, 137
computer, 7
concept, 89
conclude, 89
concludes, 128
conduct, 128
conducting, 89
conflict, 7, 17, 27, 80
conflicting, 27, 80
consequences, 109
construction, 55
consumed, 128
contradicted, 109
contradictions, 17
contrast, 81
contribute, 38, 68
contributed, 38, 68, 128
contribution, 128
contributions, 38, 68
contributors, 109
core, 17
corporations, 17
couple, 115
created, 27, 68, 109
creating, 55
creation, 27
creative, 128
credit, 89
credited, 137
cultural, 7, 37, 68, 99, 128, 137
culturally, 99
culture, 7, 17, 68, 99, 128, 137
debated, 81
decades, 109, 128
definition, 7
depressed, 81
designed, 69, 99
despite, 69, 100, 128
device, 27, 100 — *RECURSO* —
devoted, 55, 99
discrimination, 69, 109

displayed, 99 – EXPOSICIÓN – VISUALIZACIÓN — EXHIBITION
distinct, 38, 100
distinctive, 38, 137
diverse, 7, 69, 100, 128
diversity, 100
documents, 89
dominate, 100
drama, 109
dramatic, 17, 27
dramatically, 68
dynamic, 137
economic, 69, 109, 145
economy, 69, 100
edition, 55
editor, 27
effects, 109
elements, 7, 17
eliminated, 69
emerged, 37, 68
emerging, 128
emigrate, 89
emigration, 89
emphasis, 17, 100
encounter, 109 – ENCUENTRO
encountered, 38
energetic, 145
energy, 7
enhance, 81 – AUMENTAR – REALIZAR – BEAUTY
enormous, 55, 109
environment, 7, 17, 27, 89, 109 – MEDIO AMBIENTE
environmental, 27 – AMBIENTAL.
established, 37, 68, 128
ethnic, 38, 47, 68, 128
ethnicities, 38
eventually, 27, 68, 115
evident, 100
evolved, 128 – DESARROLLAR – EVOLUCIONAR
exclusion, 69
exclusively, 89
exhibitions, 109
expanded, 55
expansion, 109
expansionism, 109
expert, 81
experts, 145
exploited, 89, 109
featured, 128
features, 38, 109 – CARACTERÍSTICA – RASGO
featuring, 115

federal, 69
file, 89
final, 115
finally, 89
foundation, 27, 128
founded, 27
founder, 27
functions, 37
fundamental, 100
generation, 80
generations, 47, 128
globalization, 69
goals, 7 – METAS
grade, 7, 38
grades, 38
identical, 100
identified, 7
identify, 7, 38
ignorance, 48 – IGNORANCIA
ignored, 109
illustrate, 68
illustrates, 27
image, 109 – IMAGEN
images, 17
immigrant, 137
immigrants, 7, 37, 68, 89, 109, 128
immigrated, 27
immigration, 68
impact, 115
indicate, 48
individual, 7, 17
individualism, 7, 17, 27
individualistic, 7, 17
individuality, 17
individuals, 99
inevitable, 115
injury, 27
innovative, 27, 145
instance, 100
institutions, 7
integration, 128
intelligent, 81
intensifying, 89
involved, 27
involvement, 27 – ENREDO – COMPROMISO
isolated, 115 – AISLAR APURO
issue, 100 – CUESTIÓN – ASUNTO – PUBLICAR EMITIR
item, 89
labor, 69

laborers, 69
likewise, 38 — IGUALMENTE.
locating, 81
major, 17, 27, 37
majority, 17, 68
manipulation, 137
manual jobs, 27
mechanisms, 27
media, 17
migrated, 128
military, 69, 99
militia, 69
minimum, 89
mutually, 37
network, 100
nevertheless, 128 — SIN EMBARGO - NO OBSTANTE
notion, 128
obvious, 128
odd jobs, 27   Extraño, raro, impar.
oriented, 100
overlap, 128
parallel, 109
partnership, 27
perception, 27
period, 27
perspective, 128
perspectives, 7
phase, 137
philosopher, 55
philosophy, 27
positive, 109, 145
potential, 55
previous, 69
primary, 37
procedure, 89
publications, 89
publish, 55
published, 27, 55
publisher, 55, 128
reassess, 109
recover, 55
region, 37
regional, 100, 128
regions, 68, 100
regulated, 69
reinforce, 109
rejection, 27
reliance, 17
rely, 17

relying, 17
removal, 109
removed, 109
required, 69
resolved, 27
restored, 27
restricted, 69
restricting, 69
revealed, 115
revolution, 128
role, 17, 80, 128
route, 100
routed, 115
section, 128, 145
seeking, 89
series, 27, 55, 115
sex, 128
sexual, 128
significant, 128
similar, 55, 100
similarities, 100
specific, 69
status, 37, 80, 89, 99
straightforward, 100
stress, 81
structures, 48
style, 137
styles, 128
subculture, 7
submitted, 89
summarized, 81
summed, 69
surveys, 17
survive, 17
task, 81
teams, 89
technique, 145
technology, 69, 128
tension, 128
traced, 48, 137
tradition, 68, 128
traditional, 55, 80, 109
traditionally, 80
traditions, 7, 80, 137
transforming, 145
transport, 100
trend, 38, 137
uniform, 37
uniformity, 17, 100

unique, 55, 100, 128
variations, 37
varied, 55
varies, 100

vary, 80
visual, 145
volunteer, 55
widespread, 38, 128

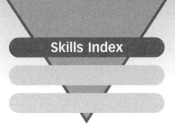

Skills Index

DISCUSSION ACTIVITIES

10–11, 18–19, 29, 40–41, 49, 56–57, 70, 82, 90–91, 102, 111, 117, 131, 139, 146

INTERNET ACTIVITIES

29, 57, 91, 117, 147

READING SKILLS

5–7, 26–27, 36–37, 46–47, 54–55, 65–68, 78–80
Comprehension, 26–27, 78–80, 136–137
Context clues, 138–139
Details, 6–7, 15, 37, 46–47, 54, 67, 88, 127, 144
Diagrams, 47
Fact vs. opinion, 108–109
Figurative language, 80
Graphs, 68
Headings, 127
Ideas of others, 126–127
Main idea, 5–6, 26, 36–37, 54, 65–67, 78, 88, 108, 114–115, 125–126, 135–136, 143–144
Poetry, 54–55
Predicting, 2, 12, 22, 32, 43, 51, 60, 74, 84, 94, 105, 112, 120, 133, 141
Prereading, 2, 12, 22, 32, 43, 51, 60, 74, 84, 94, 105, 112, 120, 133, 141
Related opinions and experiences, 16
Skimming, 136–137
Vocabulary preview, 2, 12, 22–23, 32–33, 43–44, 51–52, 60–61, 74, 84–85, 94, 105–106, 112–113, 120–121, 133, 141

TEST-TAKING SKILLS

Chronological ordering, 88
Definitions, 38–39, 101–102, 138–139
Fill in blanks, 54, 81–82, 145
Matching, 78, 98, 109, 125–126, 146
Multiple-choice questions, 5–7, 65–67, 78–79, 100–101, 117
Sentence completion, 126–127
Short-answer questions, 17–18, 55, 79–80, 88, 99, 136–137
True or false questions, 15–16, 89–90, 108–109

Test-taking Skills (*continued*)

Underlining, 108
Word finding, 7, 8–10, 16–17, 27, 37–38, 47–48, 55–56, 68–69, 80–81, 89,
    99–100, 115, 128, 137, 145

TOPICS

The American idiom, 31–57
    African American vernacular English, 44–46
    In-depth impressions, 43–46
    Languages in the United States, 33–36
    Overall impressions, 32–36
    Personal impressions, 51–53
    Student impressions, 42
    Swahili language, 42
    Walt Whitman: A man of words, 52–53
Geography and culture in the United States, 93–117
    In-depth impressions, 103–104
    Memoir of a road trip, 113–114
    Myths of the American West, 106–108
    Overall impressions, 94–104
    Personal impressions, 112–117
    Roadtrip, USA, 95–98
    Student impressions, 103–104
    Students reflect on American car culture, 103–104
Immigrant impressions, 59–91
    Immigration in the United States, 61–65
    In-depth impressions, 74–78
    It takes courage!, 70–72
    Leon Yelin: An immigrant's story, 85–87
    Overall impressions, 60–65
    Personal impressions, 83–87
    Student impressions, 70–72
    Who belongs to "Generation 1.5"?, 75–78
Musical impressions, 119–147
    American music, 121–125
    Emergence of hip-hop, 134–135
    In-depth impressions, 133–140
    Louis Armstrong: America's musical ambassador, 142–143
    Overall impressions, 120–132
    Personal impressions, 141–147
    Student impressions, 132
Values and impressions, 1–29
    American culture and values, 3–5
    American value of individualism, 13–15
    In-depth impressions, 12–15
    John Muir and conflicting American values, 23–26

Keeping to the tradition, 20–21
Overall impressions, 2–5
Personal impressions, 22–26
Student impressions, 20–21

VOCABULARY SKILLS

Academic words, 7, 16–17, 27–28, 37–38, 47–48, 55–56, 68–69, 80–81, 88–89, 99–101, 109, 115, 128, 137–138, 144
Acronyms, 48–49
Adjectives, 28, 101–102
Adverbs, 130–131
Borrowed words, 39–40
Collocations, 28, 81–82, 130–131
Confusing words, 90
Dictionary skills, 38–40, 128–130
Idiomatic phrases, 145–146
Nouns, 29, 56
Opposites, 109–110
Phrasal verbs, 110
Prepositions, 17–18, 81–82
Related words, 8–10, 116–117
Suffixes, 69
Verbs, 17–18, 81–82, 110
Visual representations, 48
Vocabulary notebook, 7, 144
Vocabulary preview, 2, 12, 22–23, 32–33, 43–44, 51–52, 60–61, 74, 84–85, 94, 105–106, 112–113, 120–121, 133, 141
Word families, 56
Word forms, 116
Word parts, 69

WRITING SKILLS

Essays, 72–73
Reading-response journal, 11, 19, 29, 41, 49–50, 57, 70, 83, 91, 102, 111, 117, 131, 139, 146
Writing topics, 11, 41, 50, 57, 72–73, 83, 91, 103, 111, 117, 131–132, 140, 146–147

Sumarrze: tell